We Shall Have Spring Again

To Georgianne

"Put on a garment of praise"

Isa 61:3

Andrée Seu

3-14-09

Also by Andrée Seu

Won't Let You Go Unless You Bless Me

Normal Kingdom Business

We Shall Have Spring Again

ESSAYS BY

Andrée Seu

WORLD & LIFE BOOKS

Essays in this book were first printed, in one form or another, as columns in *WORLD Magazine*, for which Andrée Seu is a senior writer. Some essays have been revised for this book while others remain as they were originally printed in Andrée Seu's *WORLD Magazine* column.

First World & Life Books edition published December 2008.

Book design and text composition by Matthew Mulder
Set in Zuzana Licko's Matrix II
Cover illustration by Krieg Barrie

ISBN 10: 0-9821229-2-6
ISBN 13: 978-0-9821229-2-1

Library of Congress Control Number: 2008941617

Printed in the United States of America
10 9 8 7 6 5 4 3 2 1

For
Barbara Brown,
who raised Aimée with me

CONTENTS

EDITOR'S PREFACE

We Shall Have Spring Again is organized around the theme that there are things we cannot control and, on the other hand, there are things we can do. The book begins with some heavy essays dealing with complex problems and relationships and then moves toward essays that express the believer's inevitable spirit of joy and worship, springing from trust in God's sovereignty and goodness. The title "We shall have Spring again" captures a purposeful "unquenchable optimism"—mentioned in the final chapter—that seems to secure the theme.

"Imagine that you have been cold for a very long time, as long as you can remember. You are in a snowy landscape, but this is not the pleasant kind of snow of a Thomas Kincade painting, where hot cocoa and biscuits beckon from a thatched cottage. This is the frigid, relentless white of a tundra, and you have been plying it for miles. . ."

— We Shall Have Spring Again

We Shall Have Spring Again

LIVING LOGICALLY

In the 21st century I propose to live more logically. I didn't do so well in the last one, though I had almost half of it to practice; and looking back I can't think of a single instance where it worked out better for me in the long run when I did things my way instead of His. Will any man, at the end of his life, say, "Darn it. I wish I had followed my desires instead of God's word that one time back in 1966"?

And so we find, even empirically, those of us who are God's mules, and must be controlled by bit and bridle, that sin is always destructive, always doomed, always. . . illogical.

Living logically means talking to yourself instead of listening to yourself. And when you're talking, talking Scripture. Jesus lived logically when in the wilderness he beat back each temptation with a quote from Deuteronomy.

Are you mourning? Never mind, life is short. Are you happy about that big promotion? Keep it in perspective. This "present form of this world is passing away" (I Corinthians 7:31).

Logic is what Sue L. spoke when I asked how she keeps her equanimity while raising seven kids and volunteering in the pro-life movement: "I just do the next thing that needs to be done." Wow, I thought, as I mulled it over for the next 15 years: the sovereignty of God and the responsibility of man all wrapped up and tied with a bow.

Logic is not what I saw at a Thanksgiving pageant at the local elementary school: well-scrubbed tykes performing songs of thanksgiving for sun and sky and seasons—with no one in particular to thank! Just imagine what a number that does on malleable minds just forming "logic."

I have a running argument with a friend about the bumper-sticker, "Whoever dies with the most toys wins." She insists it's serious, but I say it can only be ironic, even evangelical. (Nobody's that illogical, right?)

Logic: What do you do if someone slanders you, or otherwise abuses you? King David waxed philosophical (logical) when Abishai asked to sever the head of the seditious Shimei the Benjaminite (2 Samuel 16:10-12). It was a page from the playbook of the Greater David: "When they hurled insults at Him, He did not retaliate; when He suffered, He made no threats. Instead, He entrusted Himself to Him who judges justly" (I Peter 2:23).

Or let's say you've totally blown it—half a century used up and nothing to show for it but wood, hay, and stubble. I'm no Einstein, but it seems to me you have two logical choices here: Judas's or Peter's.

Which reminds me that related to logical living is logical praying. Daniel uses logic with God in his desperate pleading: "You have told us that you're merciful, Lord! You said it yourself! Therefore, Lord, I come to you for mercy" (chapter 9).

I am keeping two separate piles from now on, based on Deuteronomy 29:29: the things I can do something about, and the things I can't; those that belong to me, and those that belong to God. Responsibility; sovereignty.

"Sin boldly," Luther said: If you're going to choose sin and not Christ, do it whole hog. Be hot or cold but not lukewarm. I'm with him. Or with his soulmate Elijah. "If the Lord is God, follow Him; but if Baal, then follow him" (I Kings 18:21).

And logically speaking, if it turns out that Christianity isn't true, then it is the hoax of the universe. In that case I go with Paul: Let's have a party (I Corinthians 15:32). That's the logical thing. Never mind random acts of kindness. Of course we'll all be perfectly miserable because even with God dead, we just can't shake this guilt. But we can drown it in margaritas.

All right, so logical isn't in the Bible (neither is hermeneutics or Trinity). But I speak as to reasonable men. If you prefer, I can say biblical, but it's all the same to me. Christianity is more than logical, but it is at least logical, calling for the whole heart, and for the whole mind too. I stake my claim on an all-or-nothing, go-for-broke religion. And when I mess up—as I will—and lapse into the irrationality of sin, I will pray the prayer of Daniel to my God of mercy. It's only logical.

END OF THE ORDINARY

There is something insidious about the bakery. It's on my route when Spider and I take our 6 a.m. constitutional, and I spot its warmly lit window on Keswick and Mt. Carmel from a block away. Daryl's pastry shop speaks to me thusly: "There now, Andrée, I'm here. As always. And everything is all right. Those strange notions you had on your bed last night, about battles to the death in unseen spheres, and all your pretty tales, don't they seem silly by the morning's light?"

Except on Mondays. Mondays are mildly disturbing: Daryl's is closed then, and all is not right with the world. The problem is that the closing of one day is the harbinger of the closing of all days. A time will come when Daryl (who has got to be 70) will bake her last chocolate croissant and sell the business. Perhaps the Paris salon next door that's had its covetous eye on more square footage will finally prevail.

But even that will be a way station. A starker day comes: "Truly, I say to you, there will not be left here one stone upon another that will not be thrown down" (Matthew 24:2).

I lost my job two weeks ago, after eight years of making tuna-cran roll-ups. Came to work in the morning and went through the usual routines, not knowing I was executing each for the last time. An inspector arrived the same morning at the request of the bookstore above, who sought his imprimatur on new bookcases. He took one look at the 1898 structure, and at the codes, and shut us down immediately. The cheese is sliced, the wraps are thawed, and the café hum is silenced in a single hour.

We put our trust in the darnedest things. The reliability of the No. 22 bus to Willow Grove Mall. The "anchor" stores at the mall. The sun rises in the east every day and we think it is on autopilot, rather than a servant doing its rounds one more time because the Master commands it so. Someday the Master will say, "Enough. The time is come." When my husband was diagnosed with the illness that took his life, I didn't believe he would die because, well, he wasn't the type to die.

The comfort of the ordinary lulls us to a mañana state of mind. Then comes Columbine and we are shaken out of it for a week. Then comes Virginia Tech eight years later like the delayed aftershock of an earthquake. The Maker is breaking the beguilement of the ordinary and calling our attention upward:

"The Mighty One, God the Lord, speaks and summons the earth from the rising of the sun to its setting. Out of Zion, the perfection of beauty, God shines forth. Our God comes; He does not keep silence; before Him is a devouring fire, around Him a mighty tempest. He calls to the heavens above and to the earth, that He may judge His people" (Psalm 50:1-4).

There are no "ordinary days." There is always the tug of war of demons and angels, even if the battle is sometimes below the radar screen. The bucolic times in the Blue Ridge Mountains that preceded an April day of infamy were the days the plot was hatched in secret places. There are two kinds of days only: times of God's forbearance when He stays His judgment; times when He no longer stays His judgment. God says of every inch of the universe: Mine.

"All flesh is like grass and all its glory like the flower of grass. The grass withers, and the flower falls, but the word of the Lord remains forever" (1 Peter 1:24-25).

There is a liberation in that if you will have it. It works in me this way: I will put up with your bad habits if you will put up with mine. In fact, let us agree to do better than that. It's just a little while more, after all. And no longer will I be seduced by the flickering light in the flickering existence of a pastry shop.

TRUST ME

Mark Aug. 14, 2007, as the day I got tired of playing "He loves me, He loves me not." Nothing in the noumenal or phenomenal world presaged this occurrence. It was about 7 a.m. and I was walking the dog on Harrison Avenue, and at the corner of Harrison and Waverly I decided that the game stops here—which, as I think of it, is similar to C.S. Lewis's underwhelming conversion recorded in *Surprised by Joy:* "When we set out I did not believe that Jesus Christ was the Son of God, and when we reached the zoo I did."

I had been awake since 1 a.m., which is earlier by two hours than my usual waking time. It was the last stretch of a 32-hour fast in concert with a friend, we petitioning for the end of my insomnia dating from March of 2005. God's response: silence—and less sleep.

But vacillation in faith is as wearisome as sleeplessness. On 8-14-07 I was "wearied with the length of [my] way" (Isaiah 57:10). And Elijah's rebuke seemed pleasing to my soul: "How long will you go limping between two different opinions? If the Lord is God, follow Him; but if Baal, then follow him" (1 Kings 18:21).

I'm not about to lie for God. Here are the facts: "He gives to His beloved sleep" (Psalm 127:2). I am His beloved, but do not sleep. Of course there are equally embarrassing states of affair: "he who hates unjust gain will prolong his days" (Proverbs 28:16), but Jesus hated unjust gain and died at age 33. So something strange is afoot. But this is God's public-relations mess, not ours. As for us, "We cannot do anything against the truth, but only for the truth" (2 Corinthians 13:8). We are thus given liberty to say what we see, and His is the burden of wresting glory from it.

"You were born into a world at war, and you will live all your days in the midst of a great battle, involving all the forces of heaven and hell played out here on earth. . . . Until we come to terms with war as the context of our days we will not understand life. We will misinterpret 90 percent of what is happening around us and to us. It will be hard to believe that God's intentions toward us are life abundant."

(*Waking the Dead*, John Eldredge)

A certain man fasted three weeks to my one day, and not over a touch of insomnia but over visions of the "abomination that causes desolation." Was he answered speedily? He was not.

A man clothed in linen and gold touched him and said, "Fear not, Daniel, for from the first day that you set your heart to understand and humbled yourself before your God, your words have been heard, and I have come because of your words. The prince of the kingdom of Persia withstood me twenty-one days, but Michael, one of the chief princes, came to help me, for I was left there with the kings of Persia, and came to make you understand what is to happen to your people in the latter days" (Daniel 10:12-14).

Evidently, if a demon exercising influence over some foreign country gets into a tangle with your angel that God has dispatched to your rescue in response to fasting, you may sometimes have to wait a while for succor. Modern ears may tingle at this now, but if they bury the book of Daniel, they still have Ephesians 6 to contend with:

"Finally, be strong in the Lord and in the strength of His might. Put on the whole armor of God, that you may be able to stand against the schemes of the devil.

For we do not wrestle against flesh and blood, but against the rulers, against the authorities, against the cosmic powers over this present darkness, against the spiritual forces of evil in the heavenly places" (verses 10-12).

This is the best I can do with unanswered prayer. The possible answers seem to be "yes," "no," or "you have no idea what's going on behind the curtain of your sensate reality, so you best make up your mind once and for all—I do love you. Will you trust Me?"

DARKENED COUNSEL

Susanna got in the way of my having a perfect life. It's nothing she did; it's something that was done to her. Worse than that, it's something that God did to her.

Five and a half years ago, Susanna's three sons, hale men in their 20s, died in a boating mishap on the same day. Her husband and she were already divorced. Her Christian daughter subsequently renounced her faith—and her mother.

I happened to be in the home of a friend of a friend of Susanna's when the news of the accident came that spring. But I didn't know the woman. Didn't want to know her. Our paths finally crossed last month at a retreat.

A retreat, imagine. She asked to come to my room and chat. Just before that, a woman in the last session had raised her hand and asked how we can be joyful when we're always "waiting for the other shoe to drop."

I offered sound theology: "Is anyone among you suffering? Let him pray. Is anyone cheerful? Let him sing praise" (James 5:13). Someone else did better: "Life is like a fairy tale where a lot of bad things happen in the middle, but the ending is happy. Think about the ending."

Sitting in my room with Susanna, I gave up all thought of saying a helpful word, though that's why she had come. I was scandalized myself. I felt like David when God struck Uzzah because he touched the ark. "David was angry because the Lord had burst forth against Uzzah. . . . And David was afraid of the Lord that day" (2 Samuel 6:8-9). God had killed the hapless cart man in the middle of a worship dance to the accompaniment of "songs and lyres and harps and tambourines and castanets and cymbals."

Susanna does not fit in my theology. She is like Psalm 88, a chapter of the Bible that you always hope won't be there next time you open it. Some other Psalms start poorly but have soaring endings. Psalm 88 has no ray of hope.

At one point in the retreat I had read selections from *Children's Letters to God:*

"Dear God, In school they told us what you do.

Who does it when you're on vacation? Erin"

"Dear God, Instead of letting people die and having to make new ones why don't you just keep the ones you got now? Jane"

"Dear God, If you let the dinosaur not extinct we would not have a country. You did the right thing. Jonathan"

"Dear God, If you give me a genie lamp like Alladin, I will give you anything you want except my money or my chess set. Raphel"

What makes the letters cute is that the kids are clueless and yet they're giving God advice.

I went home and read all of Job.

God gave Job no answers. Nor did He apologize. He is God; He does as He pleases. We are all clueless, like children, and yet would give Him advice. He tells us that He is good. There is nothing to do with that but accept it or reject it. Job's wife rejected it, as did Susanna's daughter: "Curse God and die," they said. That's a choice.

I told two of my friends, independently of each other, the story of Susanna, thinking I would rattle their faith too, thinking I was presenting them with a theological Gordian Knot. I thought we would do a little hand-wringing together and flirting with doubts. They surprised me and said, in effect, "It all comes down to trusting Him."

Writer Anne Lamott tells the story of a little boy locked in his room and afraid. But his mother reaches under the door and finds his fingers, and he is consoled enough to wait for the locksmith who's coming in a while. This is the best we will do with Susanna: God's presence and His promise.

"Who is this that darkens counsel by words without knowledge?" (Job 38:2). That would be me, Lord.

"I know that you can do all things, and that no purpose of yours can be thwarted. 'Who is this that hides counsel without knowledge?' Therefore I have uttered what I did not understand, things too wonderful for me, which I did not know" (Job 42:2-3).

A LITTLE KINDNESS, PLEASE

A saying on the office door of a professor here at seminary: "For every complex problem, there is an answer that is clear, easy, elegant, and wrong." Methinks it should be taped over every classroom, nailed to the lintel of every domicile, and sandblasted into the granite of church porticos across the land.

Not always right but never in doubt, that's us. Name an issue and we line up with an opinion. Organic eggs versus nonorganic? Not only do I have a view on this, but if yours is different from mine, I like you a little less somehow.

Silverware up or down in the dish drainer? I used to be a big "down" person—because of the obvious danger of self-impaling. At age 54 I became a big "up" person—because of the obvious hygiene considerations of blades in contact with accumulated dinner detritus at the base of said drainer (and because my friend told me he does it that way).

No controversy is too small. But the bigger they are the harder our unity falls. Here's a medium-sized issue that came up before Valentine's Day: I asked my daughter if her boyfriend has ever sent her a Valentine. She said no in a way that I discerned—notwithstanding her militant anti-commercialism and subscription to *Adbusters* magazine—that she lamented the annual oversight.

So, do I phone Tim with a hot tip that could save a relationship? Or do I refrain? I can argue it both ways. Scripture says, "Do unto others as you would have them do unto you." Well, if I were my daughter, I would absolutely not appreciate FTD flowers forthcoming from a feckless suitor who needed prompting by Mama. On the other hand, if I were Tim, I would be most grateful. Which is the way of love? I'll bet you have a firm opinion on that.

I see in the papers that a federal lawsuit has ignited over a local schoolboy's donning of a Jesus costume in a school parade last Halloween. The principal said to ditch the paper crown of thorns and call the robe a Roman toga. The boy and mother demurred, reasoning that if devils and vampires could prance the corridors of public education, why shouldn't the Lord of Lords? How say you, reader?

Do you give a handout to a street beggar? I thought it was a good thing, till a woman I respect who works in a private city shelter told me that it undermines her colleagues' efforts to coax service-resistant homeless to give up their alleys and parks. What say you, reader? The situation is a bit more complex than I thought when I was cocksure.

On a Thursday I had dinner with a couple who persuaded me by the end of the chicken cordon bleu that it's insanity to support a U.S. missionary to the tune of $100,000 when we can help a dozen indigenous gospel laborers who already know the language and culture. On a Friday I had dinner with a former missionary to Madras who persuaded me that though it might seem more cost-effective to just send money, there are good reasons to also send warm bodies abroad: (1) It is important for our affluent American souls to guard that personal connection to the Great Commission and not a mere arms-length, monetary one; (2) it is important for cross-pollination of insight to have culture sharpen culture. What say you, reader? Complex and inelegant, eh?

On war, what say you? I used to say it was wrong for us to get into country A because we're not offering the same help to countries B through M, which also have evil dictators. Then I recognized the false antithesis in my argument: Just because we can't help all doesn't mean we shouldn't help some.

In *The Great Divorce*, the shining Spirit divulges one of heaven's secrets to an earthling still stuck on loveless opinionism: "That's what we all find when we reach this country. We've all been wrong! That's the great joke. There's no need to go on pretending one was right! After that we begin living."

The Lord "knows the secrets of the heart" (Psalm 44:21) and that's what He cares about. Doctrine is good and love is better. How about a little kindness, please?

DEPENDENCE DAY

I've been waiting for the day when I can amass just enough spiritual capital to achieve some independence and not have to go begging God for every little thing.

I have envisioned what it would look like: I would have read enough of the great books to be respectable in polite society. I would be over the sleep slump that leaves me stupid with exhaustion. I would have attained enough competence in some skill area to "amount to something." I would possess surplus of purity of heart the way I have stockpiles of paper towels in the pantry, not having to fight for it anew every day in prayer.

I always think it's just around the corner, this restful coasting. In the meantime, I'm constantly desperate for God. "Here comes Andrée again, asking for a clean heart," He must say. (Once my son

Jae dropped in at the café and watched fascinated as two students prayed at least five minutes before their meal. "God must be looking at His watch," he whispered wryly.)

There are precedents to my frustration in the tale of that other widow, from Zarephath, and don't think I haven't noted the similarity. A stranger blows into town and asks for bread. "I have nothing baked, only a handful of flour in a jar and a little oil in a jug. And now I am gathering a couple of sticks that I may go in and prepare it for myself and my son, that we may eat it and die" (1 Kings 17:12). She is already counting herself dead.

At this point Elijah can, if he wants to, call on Jehovah Jireh to throw open the storerooms of heaven and make it rain fig cakes. But he does not. He promises only, "The jar of flour shall not be spent, and the jug of oil shall not be empty, until the day that the Lord sends rain upon the earth." Every day she comes down to the kitchen (Is she biting her fingernails?) and there is just a little meal and a little oil, enough for the day.

We like a little more margin than that, thank you very much. But God is not into comfort zones. He dispatches disciples to preach with "no staff, nor bag, nor bread, nor money" (Luke 9:3). His heavenly caterers send manna enough for the day, but try to scrape up Wednesday's dinner on Tuesday and you'll get maggoty manna for your unbelief (Exodus 16:20). Lesson: God will be as faithful on Wednesday as He was on Tuesday.

David commissioned the troops of Israel to be counted so he could put his confidence in numbers, and even commander Joab (no paragon of virtue) thought it was a bad idea.

Recently I counted all the essays I have stockpiled over the years. They were a buffer against writer's block, a safety net in case the Lord did not come through, a comfort zone in which the comfort was not having to rely on God. Maggoty, every one—stale and dated. Each one taking hours to write, each one representing time I didn't spend with my kids, they fall under Joshua's condemnation over the rebuilding of Jericho: "At the cost of his firstborn shall he lay its foundations, and at the cost of his youngest son shall he set up its gates" (Joshua 6:26).

Simon the Sorcerer (Acts 8) is merely the crassest illustration of my desire to own the gifts of God as a commodity. Who needs moment-by-moment relationship with God? Just sell me ownership of the

Holy Spirit to wield independently of Him. To me be the glory!

I am chastened but happy. Begging God daily is the right place to be. Not to possess anything in myself but to draw the day's grace as the branch draws from the vine—whether bread or essays or purity of heart. Andrew Murray says it was God's intention, in creating the universe, to communicate His attributes to His creatures:

"But this communication was not meant to give created beings something they could possess in themselves, having full charge and access apart from Him. Rather, God as the ever-living, ever-present, ever-acting One, . . . meant that the relationship of His creatures to Himself would be one of unceasing, absolute dependence" (Humility).

In your right mind you wouldn't want it any other way.

CONFIDENCE, NOT CERTAINTY

I hope you will accept a New Year's revolution in lieu of a New Year's resolution. I want to share one of the most helpful things I have learned. It concerns liberation from the fallacy of 100 percent.

Let me explain that I have long experienced a troubling gap between my theology and my life. The Bible just doesn't reach where the rubber meets the road. It says I am given "all things I need for life and godliness," but my opinion has been that I am given only "some things." I find in Scripture general principles like "love your neighbor," "be slow to speak," and "do not cast pearls to swine."

General principles are fine if you live in a general world. But I live in an insistently specific world where the issues are:

"Should I take this job?" "Should I marry this man?" "Should I skip writing today to be with my

Mom?" "Should I let Calvin learn on the stick shift?" "Christian school or homeschool?" "Milk without the bovine growth hormones and antibiotics at $4.19/ half gallon, or with the undesirables at $1.95/half gallon?"

"Should I have that neighborhood open house, hoping to 'sow seeds'—and trust God with the money?" "How many missionaries do I have time to pray for?" "Should I continue to drag to church a 14-year-old who is hostile to the gospel?" (The case for "yes" is that it is at least exposure to the gospel; the case for "no" is that repeated rejections of the gospel heap judgment.)

For these and about 50 questions a day, I have felt I need more information in order to proceed with assurance. I have become weary of doing just about everything I do with no rock-solid certainty of its rightness. In fact, if truth be told, the state of affairs induces paralysis and a low-grade depression.

In October I had the pleasure of interviewing Dr. Vern Poythress of Westminster Seminary. He gave me two delicious hours and we ended up talking about the Holy Spirit. I was sharing with him a Beth Moore insight, in which she compared the work of the Spirit in us—His "resonating" with our spirit (Romans 8:16;

1 Corinthians 2)—to the resonating of all the "C" strings of a piano when middle "C" is struck.

That's when he said the words that liberated: "Many times the resonance of the Spirit is thought of as being passive," said Dr. Poythress, "but He calls on us to be creative because He is sovereign. . . . A trust in God says, 'I'm going to venture on this. I know my motives are not perfect but I'm going to try it because I know God loves me.'" The Spirit in us gives us "freedom of exploration."

The Bible is not a Middle Ages casuistry book that attempts to cover every conceivable ethical situation. Moreover, there are "disputable matters," unclear matters, in the Christian life (Romans 14:1). God could clear them up with a word if He wanted to, but He chooses not to. And so our decisions are not always wrought with 100 percent certainty. And that's OK.

I had been laboring under a fallacy—the fallacy of 100 percent certainty. I can be certain that Jesus loves me, but I do not possess the same order of certainty that He wants me to have a Mercedes.

But if I (1) investigate a matter thoroughly and (2) inquire of the Lord for guidance, then even though a postcard doesn't drop from heaven with an unequivocal answer, I can move forward with a spiritual commodity that is more true to the real world than "certainty"—"confidence."

Confidence that God loves me. Confidence that His Spirit lives in me. Confidence that if I make a mistake His arms will be there to catch this frail saint and put her back on righteous paths, for His name's sake. This new year and the next.

THREE-TWO-ONE

There are three kinds of fools by my reading of Proverbs. There is the fist-shaking fool who knows not at Whom he rants and raves: "Come with us, let us lie in wait for blood; let us ambush the innocent without reason; like Sheol let us swallow them alive, and whole, like those who go down to the pit" (Proverbs 1:11-12). Of his number are those who "cannot sleep unless they have done wrong; they are robbed of sleep unless they have made someone stumble" (Proverbs 4:16).

The second is the fool whose turpitude does not even rise to the level of interesting sin, but he sinks in his torpor, slouches in his sloth, and wallows in his middling wantonness. He commits adultery, not so much out of highhanded rebellion as ennui: He falls in with "the forbidden woman . . . the adulteress with her smooth words, who forsakes the companion of her youth and forgets the covenant of her God" (Proverbs 2:16-17). Also in this pretty kettle of fish is he who "follows worthless pursuits" (Proverbs 12:11) and the slothful man who "will not roast his game" (Proverbs 12:27). (There is bleeding between the categories.)

The third fool is the one who "means well" but is ignorant of the law, or of his times, or of his very heart. My own children, when ensnared, are wont to plead ignorance as innocence, but I tell them we have manslaughter as well as murder on the books, and both are punishable. Ignorance is culpable when you should have known better, and when by a thousand culpable past choices you failed to apprise yourself of the state of things. This fool is the "simple" man (Proverbs 14:15); he is the man not paying attention. He is the one Jesus rebuked for not knowing his times (Matthew 16:3).

It seems to me I have often dabbled in categories 1 and 2 with far less outward consequence than has been recently meted on me by a category 3, which this fall cost me my job. (I sent small class pictures of my students to a prayer partner who is in prison.)

There are two kinds of choices when you are found in a life implosion, and suicide is one of them.

On that track there is the swift kind, favored by Judas and Ahithophel, and the protracted, popular method—denial, alcohol, television stupor. Or you simply say to yourself, "I messed up so bad I won't even bother trying to do right anymore. What's the use?"

The alternative is to remember that the fundamental things apply in cataclysms as well as calm times. To wit: Do the right thing; one foot in front of the other; one piece of the problem at a time; take lunch, exercise, sleep. I remember the counselor Jay Adams saying that the trouble is not usually that we don't know what to do but that we don't do it long enough. We give up just before the breakthrough would have come. Like Screwtape said, "It is so hard for these creatures to persevere." But persevering is what it's all about. Persevering is just faith with Nikes on.

There is One who saves from all my folly, no questions asked. There is One who knows that I committed at least 10 worse sins the day I got fired than the sin that brought me down: I coveted, I lusted, I gossiped, I judged, I lied to avoid some unpleasantness, I neglected my kids, I was lazy, I drove so as to endanger. For none of these was I subjected to public opprobrium; for none did I blanket the town with apologies. He it is I trust with the mind-boggling asymmetry of consequences.

Praise be to God who sorts all things out with justice, so that we need not overly exert ourselves with bloviated self-defense. My conscience is clear but that does not make me innocent (1 Corinthians 4:4). Jesus's conscience was clear and He was innocent. He did not agitate but "continued entrusting Himself to the One who judges justly" (1 Peter 2:23). And if it's good enough for Him it's good enough for me.

CONFESSIONS OF A PROOFREADER

I have no confidence in history. I don't mean the stuff Santayana says we should remember, or we're condemned to repeat it. I mean the books—the digested, scripted, packaged and bound, authorized version of things.

It wasn't always like this with me. Not that I swallowed great gulps of the Peloponnesian Wars in high school. And I admit it's my fault, not St. Clare High's, that in my 50s I suffer recurring cold-sweat dreams about running out of semester before running out of Palmer & Colton's *A History of the Modern World.*

I married and my husband liked history. Liked it well enough to write a 600-page dissertation on the 20th-century Korean church, which he had me proofread. Here is where my sordid tale begins.

The job description was simple enough: "Just fix

the grammar."

Even those of us who are French Canadians wed to Koreans should be able to manage that. Or so I thought. Just cross out every place you find "the," insert "the" every place you don't. Change "r" to "l" and vice versa, as in "probrem." (My husband wrote like he talked.)

I wouldn't say I'm an especially trusting person. I tend to test every word my neighbors say, putting out a tentative toe for land mines before offering myself, doing a little excavation before exposing my own foibled personality.

But when it comes to language, to the printed text, I plunged ahead with all the faith of a Calvin, expecting it to hold me up, to lead me where it promises.

Picture a page of print. Suddenly, in a preview of the Apocalypse, all the coordinating conjunctions are raptured. You are left without a compass in the thicket of a history with names like Kwang Suk Suh and Kidok Shinbo and Pasoo Koon. You feel betrayed by dependent clauses that lead you along through a string of commas, then right up against the brick wall of a period.

More flexible people would catch on to the flow

of a sentence where just one comma's out of place. But I plead your indulgence:

Losing that, war was inevitable.

Losing that war was inevitable.

More optimistic people would make it a game. A sort of Rubik's Cube. An Easter egg hunt for modes of relationship— Causality? Chronology? Sequentiality? Opposition? Apposition? Contingency?

Not me. I burst into the study, to an unsuspecting spouse, thrust the paper in his hand and challenge, "Here, YOU read that!"—already gloating in my victory. Unruffled, he proceeds. Placidly, he finishes: "What's the probrem?"

OK, I go for Rubik's Cube, peppering pages with judicious applications of . . .

"Still, . . ."

"Notwithstanding . . ."

"By corollary, . . ."

"Parenthetically, . . ."

"Nevertheless, . . ."

"Specifically, . . ."

"More to the point, . . ."

And slowly, ever so slowly, flecks of gold emerge from the dross. Inside my husband's head, behold, there is a logic crying to come out.

People who have tried it know there's a fine line between editing and creating content; the one is a respectable service, the other cheating. (I'd better figure out the difference soon: With the café behind me, I'll no doubt be doing more proofreading.) But what do you do, I pray you, when a quoted Dr. Park "says" 150 times in a row? After a while, one is tempted to make him "intone," to "demur," to "report," even (heaven help me) to "pontificate."

I became more daring, positing states of emotion, guessing at personality traits, filling in gaps:

"Jubilantly, . . ."

"Not surprisingly, . . ."

"With characteristic humility . . ."

I thought of all the people who might read this dissertation. Would they be word-trusters like me? Would they put too much confidence in my descriptive embellishments and absorb them into their worldviews?

I thought of all the footnotes (there are hundreds), all the authors that my husband quoted, trusted, rested on for his own enlightenment. Every one with proofreaders, every one with deadlines, every one subject to fatigue, ego, and homoeoteleuton. I mean, how does the Fall affect all this, anyhow?

My husband might have been right that I'm neurotic. But I now read *Newsweek* editorials with a jaundiced eye, not the same person I was. Still, I am weighing what he said. What's in a comma, after all? The divine Being over us will overrule all our errors. Or is it: The Divine, being over us, will overrule all our errors?

IN YOUR FACE

C.S. Lewis's *The Magician's Nephew* brings us to a strange world beyond 1940s England. Digory and Polly come upon the ruin of a once gala banquet hall in which are seated hundreds of frozen figures, all magnificently robed and crowned—which is what catches Polly's eye.

"But Digory was more interested in the faces. . . . You could walk down and look at the faces in turn. 'They were nice people, I think,' said Digory. . . . Both the men and women looked kind and wise, and they seemed to come of a handsome race. But after the children had gone a few steps down the room they came to faces that looked a little different. These were very solemn faces. You felt you would have to mind your P's and Q's, if you ever met living people who looked like that.

"When they had gone a little further, they found

themselves among faces they didn't like: this was about the middle of the room. The faces here looked very strong and proud and happy, but they looked cruel. A little further on they looked crueller. Further on again, they were still cruel but they no longer looked happy. They were even despairing faces: as if the people they belonged to had done dreadful things and also suffered dreadful things. The last figure of all was the most interesting—a woman even more richly dressed than the others . . . with a look of such fierceness and pride that it took your breath away."

I have been thinking about faces. I remember the first time I saw Marge Magnuson's face. I was 23 and hippie-grungy and plopped on her doorstep, some vagabond accompanying her "adopted son." She opened the door and looked at me—and beamed. That was my introduction to Christianity.

I remember other, less pleasant, kinds of faces, and I have worn those. Passing judgment on Israel, God says, "For the look on their faces bears witness against them" (Isaiah 3:9). Seeking her repentance one more time before judgment falls, He appeals through Hosea: "Plead with your mother, plead . . . that she put away her whoring from her face" (Hosea 2:2). Most do not respond in repentance, of course: "They have made their faces harder than rock" (Jeremiah 5:3). Some newsstand magazine faces should be blushing at this but Jeremiah says, "They did not know how to blush" (Jeremiah 6:15).

If you ever need a cure for lust, read this encounter between a saint and a damned soul in *The Great Divorce:* "I think the most pitiable was a female Ghost. . . . [She] seemed quite unaware of her phantasmal appearance. More than one of the Solid People tried to talk to her, and at first I was quite at a loss to understand her behaviour to them. She appeared to be contorting her all but invisible face and writhing her smokelike body in a quite meaningless fashion.

"At last I came to the conclusion—incredible as it seemed—that she supposed herself still capable of attracting them and was trying to do so. She was a thing that had become incapable of conceiving conversation save as a means to that end. If a corpse already liquid with decay had arisen from the coffin, smeared its gums with lipstick, and attempted a flirtation, the result could not have been more appalling. In the end she muttered 'Stupid creatures,' and turned back to the bus."

Ah, but then there is Stephen, so filled with the

Spirit that at his kangaroo court trial, "Gazing at him, all who sat in the council saw that his face was like the face of an angel" (Acts 6:15).

I have started asking God for a face like that, a face like the visages of the 24 elders encircling the throne on better thrones than the ones Polly and Digory saw, faces gleaming white because they always look upon the Lamb at the center. When I walk Spider, my face is the first thing people see of me. Do we pass without a gospel word in this shortness of time, or might my face pour forth speech—leading sometimes to second and third things?

LOGIC! WHY DON'T THEY TEACH LOGIC?

Reading 142 high-school essays a week (my summer job) is like overhearing one end of a phone conversation: You can tell what's being said on the other end by what's filtering through on yours. I haven't set foot in the classroom of this SAT preparation school except to pick up and drop off on Tuesdays and Fridays, but it took only the first few bluebooks to discern the test-busting formulas dispensed in Ms. G's room.

The Educational Testing Service in its redoubtable wisdom (and perhaps in capitulation to California higher learning institutions, which threatened in 2001 to drop the admissions criteria as culturally outmoded) added in 2005 a 25-minute writing section to the already-dreaded College Board bugbear. Lucky for me I took the thing in 1968 because I would score 0 on a possible 6 today, turning in a blank page save for neurotic scribbles of horses.

Do you have any idea how long it takes me to write an essay? First I have to have all the dishes done and the beds made, I need to have a glass of water, to pace, and to check all my email. Anne Lamott has a chapter in *Bird by Bird* devoted solely to "Lousy First Drafts," except she doesn't use the word "lousy."

Therefore one cannot be too self-righteous toward an SAT prep school when one realizes it is devoted to ways of beating the system rather than to teaching good writing. (I am reminded of the question posed by a lackey in Cruella DeVil's fashion design emporium in *101 Dalmatians:* "Do we like stripes this year?")

Evidently, to go by Ms. G's classroom essays, the "stripes" that the College Board judges like this year are as follows: statement of opinion and quick mentions of two supporting examples in paragraph 1, elaboration on said examples in subsequent paragraphs. This could conceivably work, I suppose. But a technique, like a gun, in the hands of someone not properly trained will misfire. Edmond Rostand undoubtedly had the SAT writing section in mind when in 1897 he penned the scene in Cyrano de Bergerac where the handsome but uninspired Christian woos Roxane in her balcony with poetry whispered to him by the homely but talented Cyrano behind the bushes. The delivery is laughably wooden. All of this will have to be deprogrammed in college or journalism school.

Here are two typical samples in answer to the assigned topic question, "Do people achieve more by cooperation than by competition?":

Sample 1: "People should always cooperate to get what they want. In American history, America became independent due to its cooperation with the French. In *A Separate Peace* by John Knowles, the main characters Gene and Finny exemplify the dark side of competition. Thus, cooperation should be preferred over competition."

Sample 2: "I agree that people can achieve more by cooperation rather than competition. From the democracy formed by kids in *Lord of the Flies* to the sailor Edmund Dantes in *The Count of Monte Cristo*, people achieve more through cooperation." (*Lord of the Flies* comes up a lot in this stack I'm grading; the book must be having a renaissance.)

"Logic!" said the Professor half to himself. "Why don't they teach logic at these schools?"

Answer to the Professor: The College Board reader will spend one minute on each essay, so other qualities of writing are more imperative for

Ms. G—notably length. Les Perelman of M.I.T. studied the new test and got good at guessing a student's score by how long the essay was, even from across the room! Perelman concluded about the exercise, "It does harm," and exclaimed, "Chase the money changers from the temple!" of academia. (Well, he's assuming the rest of academia isn't neck deep in the same mire.)

Perelman's Bible quote is my segue into the most disheartening observation of all: I don't know these kids but I know their parents. They're Christians, or at least they go to doctrinally sound churches. But there is nary a trace of a Christian perspective in any of the 142 essays I read. This is either another deliberately inculcated SAT-taking strategy to pander to the Princeton reader, or it is evidence of a thought compartmentalization that divorces critical thinking from biblical thinking. I don't know which is worse.

Next suggested essay writing topic: "Is it better to gain the world and to lose your soul?"

A NOTE FROM GOD

I have in my possession a note from God that I brought home from Glade Springs, Texas. It's in pencil block print and the signature is unmistakable: "God."

The message reads, "I love you. I will never leave you. Do not be afraid. You are beautiful." A little girl in Sunday finery who furtively passed it to me, all neatly folded, slipped into the crowd before I could inquire, but I know it was authentic because I read my Bible every day and the note says all the things He says: "I love you"—John 3:16; "I will never leave you"—Hebrews 13:5; "Do not be afraid"—Luke 12:7; "You are beautiful"—Philippians 2:15.

At the Glade I had stepped into the pages of 1 Corinthians 14, as if 2,000 years between were but a day. "When you come together, each one has a hymn, a lesson, a revelation, a tongue, or an interpretation. Let all things be done for building up. . . . Let two or three prophets speak, and let the others weigh what is said. If a revelation is made to another sitting there, let the first be silent. For you can all prophesy one by one, so that all may learn and all be encouraged."

This is what I found that Sunday morning, all "done decently and in order," "the spirits of the prophets subject to prophets." Here are workaday, lunch-pail-toting believers in first-century Corinth and in 21st-century Texas worship services speaking to the brethren "for their upbuilding and encouragement and consolation" (which Paul suggests is the essence of prophecy), and it's all new to this know-it-all northerner.

Now since that July in 2005 I have seen prophecies that were wrong and prophecies that were right. I have also heard sermons that were wrong and sermons that were right. Neither should be taken as revelation and both can be botched, but why should we expect perfection of gifts in fallible men?

Turns out sometimes the prophecy is right and the conclusion is wrong. In Tyre godly disciples advised Paul through the Spirit not to go to Jerusalem. And in Caesarea Agabus prophesied by the Spirit that the Jews would bind Paul in Jerusalem and turn him over to the Gentiles, and urged him not to go. Paul went anyway—in the Spirit—and the rest is history. What happened? They both heard right about the suffering; they just disagreed as to the conclusion for action.

I realize prophecy is a theological hot potato. If I were having coffee with a Presbyterian I would say, "Let's open our minds to the whole Bible and not gerrymander certain gifts out of the list of gifts named in 1 Corinthians 12." If I were having coffee with a Charismatic I would say, "Let's broaden our view of prophecy and define it as all kinds of wise and godly advice from all kinds of Christians who might not even know there is such a thing as prophecy in this day and age."

Rev. Tim Keller (a Presbyterian) says, "There is a vitality in the Corinthian church. . . . There is a new level of ministry now that we're in the Pentecostal era because the Holy Spirit has come down. . . . In the New Testament suddenly we see the word 'prophet' all over the place. Everybody wants to give an exhortation. . . . Paul says, when the prophets are done, evaluate them. He doesn't say, when 1 Corinthians is read, evaluate it. In other words, Apostolic revelation evaluates prophecy."

So, if someone comes to you and says, "The Lord told me you should date that girl," I suggest you go home and think about it but don't have your conscience bound by it. Or you could always reply, "The Lord told me different"—and then go sit down and talk about it like two Christian adults with wisdom.

1 Thessalonians 5:20-21 says, "Do not despise prophecies, but test everything." God communicates with us in many ways, even through little girls in country churches. Let the spirits of the prophets be unhindered. Let the written Word of the closed canon judge all claims to revelation.

MINISTER AND NOT MANIPULATE

Twenty-three years ago (mothers can date everything by the ages of their children) I received, in exchange for babysitting, a book titled *The Marriage Builder* by Larry Crabb. His two-word contrast— minister versus manipulate—always stuck with me, even when I was not actively employing it.

The genius of Crabb's formulation is the insight that at any given moment, I am either ministering to you or manipulating you. There is no third way. All that is not ministry is manipulation; all that is not manipulation is ministry. And because there are only the two possibilities, self-examination of motives is made easy.

The question when examining "You are pretty," or "I'm tired" is what impact these statements of mine have on you, my hearer. Does it benefit you to be told this? Does it minister to your soul in a godly way, or does it deceive you, heap guilt on you, extract a service from you? "Minister" forces me to do some hard thinking—that would be good for this person I live with or work with?

We could simply call the thing "love" and be done with it, for that is what it is. But "love" has nowadays been confused with romance, and what we have in mind is made of "sterner stuff," as Mark Antony would say. So it is good to have recourse to other words. There is nothing particularly romantic about "ministering" a needed rebuke to a friend, or calling a spouse on a sin, or listening to a sad story when you just want to go to bed, There is nothing of Cupid's bliss in holding your tongue when you would rather lacerate with it.

Jesus's interactions with the Pharisees are a textbook illustration of ministry versus manipulation—them forever trying to catch Him, hurt Him, kill Him, for what they perceive is the best long-term interest; Him forever being straight with them, telling them the truth, though He knows it will cost His life.

What surprises about ministering is the benefit it accrues to the one who chooses to minister rather than manipulate. There is a saying that no one works harder than the lazy person. Similarly, no one has less peace than the manipulator. He is always focused on himself, which as we know is the recipe of death. ("The mind of sinful man is death," Romans 8:6.) One is never so free as when getting one's mind off the self and onto another's welfare. The self-involved soul is a casket, as C.S. Lewis reminded us "airless, care-less, impervious to all of love's arrows, impervious to love iteself."

Ministry to others unleases blessing because to minister is a command of God, and God watches over His commands to bless them. Startlingly, the commands of His that at first glance would seem to be the most onerous turn out to be the very doorways to joy. "Whoever would save his life will lose it, but whoever loses his life for my sake will save it" (Luke 9:24).

Life has enough complications. The phrase "minister and not manipulate" is not too taxing for my mind. Many times a day, as often as the ship of my soul veers off into its natural bent of manipulation, this shorthand comes back to me and sets my rudder straight. It works only by faith, by taking God at His word, and believing that He is, and He rewards those who earnestly seek Him. But that goes without saying, right? Otherwise, who would ever minister if you could just manipulate?

A SYMBOL OF GLORY

I will write precisely one column on this, and one column is all it deserves. I have taken to wearing a head covering during worship. I expect one in a thousand readers follows this practice, so you might all be annoyed with me.

If this were the '50s, you would simply say "So what?" to my haute couture confession. All women—even Protestants—sported hats on Sunday morning, though as the Cheshire Cat's smile on a long-faded piety. I remember that JFK killed the male hat industry. I'm not sure what killed the distaff counterpart; all I know is back then hats were worn to church because hats were worn to church.

I was not on a campaign against or for anything, although I admit that Dietrich Bonhoeffer has marked me in some way I can't shake. Speaking of revival he said: "There arises a more determined quest for Him

Who is the sole object of it all, for Jesus Christ Himself. What did Jesus mean to say to us? . . . What we want to know is not, what would this or that man, or this or that Church, have of us, but what Jesus Christ Himself wants of us" (*The Cost of Discipleship*).

I'm having a revival. It's been going on about three years, though it took a while to notice, just as you don't realize a radiator has warmed your room till it's been happening a while. My personal great awakening involves "a more determined quest for Him who is the sole object of it all." This means trying "to discern what is pleasing to the Lord" (Ephesians 5:10), even when it's baffling.

It means launching out and putting a symbol of "glory" on my head at church because I think 1 Corinthians 11 tells me to, even if I may turn out in the end to be wrong. That's because I will definitely be wrong if I don't do what I think God is commanding. To disobey what I think God is telling me is to disobey God. There is nothing more a man can do at any given moment than say yes to God as he hears Him. It is God Himself who gently steers our boats, and corrects their course, but only as we're moving toward Him (Philippians 3:15-16).

Granted, "Let her cover her head" (1 Corinthians

11:6) may not be as important as "pour yourself out for the hungry" (Isaiah 58:10)—if you can call any part of God's Word unimportant. But I figure if the king tells you to go conquer the hinterlands one day, and tells you to shoe his horse the next day, you should do them both without slacking. He is the king.

There's a lot more than mantillas at stake for me personally. I want to stop putting filters between me and the Word of God. I appreciate scholarship, but it is rarely conclusive. The question is this: When push comes to shove, do I go with Christian peer pressure or with God's Word as I see it? All my obediences to received practice are suspect when I balk at the one point where conscience makes a contrary demand. It's when there is disjunction that my true allegiance shows.

I read in 1 Corinthians 11 that the woman's head is to be covered in worship. The modern Christian consensus tells me that is a relative and obsolete command, dealing with some first-century problem in the city of Corinth. My high-school literary skills tell me otherwise: The command is rooted in creation (verses 7-9) and in nature (verse 14). And if that weren't ironclad enough, I am to cover my head "because of the angels."

The angel detail is so cryptic, so off the wall, so without explanation, that it becomes the strongest argument of all. Where is the "cultural relativity" case now, where angels transcend all historical agitations?

The Apostle Paul says there are some convictions we best keep between ourselves and God (Romans 14:22). Maybe head covering is one of those. The saleslady ringing up my little black lacy number at the Catholic shop asked if I was going to Rome. I didn't want to get into it with her, but I've gone into it with you, for better or worse. Just for one column, though, which is no doubt all it deserves.

THE THING WE DON'T DO

Forgiving is the hardest thing you will ever do. That's why most people don't do it. We talk about it, cheer for it, preach on it, and are sure we've practiced it. But mostly the illusion of having forgiven is that the passage of time dulls memory. The ruse will come to light with hair-trigger vengeance when fresh offense hurls in to empty out the gunnysack of half-digested grievances.

I asked a few people if they'd ever forgiven anyone, and what it felt like. They gave me answers so pious I knew they'd never done it. I am at the present moment in the maw of temptation, and I can tell you there is nothing exalted about this feeling, this one-two punch to the gut that comes when you even contemplate forgiving, which is as far as I've come.

At first I decided I would forgive the person—and

never speak to him again. This felt pretty good, but I saw the dissimulation in it at once. I alternately toyed with going to him to "tell him his fault" (Matthew 18:15), which is my biblical right, so there. I had the decree of rebuke written up in my head, a document of fastidious and plenary detail—all for his own good. A smarmy satisfaction accompanied the plan, so I nixed it. For now.

In C.S. Lewis's *The Great Divorce*, a woman confronted by an angel about forgiving her husband says, "Well, I have forgiven him as a Christian." The phrase is meaningless. She then bulimically seethes for pages about his wrongdoing and her longsuffering.

Keeping one's mouth shut is commendable, and more than I have managed in the past. It will work as long as I don't go near a phone or e-mail. But I am reminded that "Absalom spoke to Amnon neither good nor bad" for two whole years after the rape of his sister Tamar, and it ate him alive till in the end he killed the man.

O my brothers, you cannot imagine the exquisite verbal retaliations I have hatched in the idle hours, each more perfect than the last: theologically impeccable, legalistically faultless, poisoned prose polished to a lethal point. Must I now relinquish these? Must I kill the little darlings? Are they not to see the light of day? Such a waste.

Forgiveness is a brutal mathematical transaction done with fully engaged faculties. It's my pain instead of yours. I eat the debt. I absorb the misery I wanted to dish out on you, and you go scot-free. Beware the forgiveness that is tendered soon after injury; be suspicious. Real forgiveness needs a time lag, for it is wrought in private agony before it ever comes to public amnesty. All true acts of courage are thus done in secret.

Pastor Tim Keller of Redeemer Church in Manhattan shares the following letter from a man who once had to forgive a woman:

"I forgave her and it took me a whole year and I had to forgive her in small sums over that whole twelve months. I paid those sums whenever I spoke to her and kept myself from rehashing the past. I paid them whenever I saw her with another man and refused self-pity and rehearsal inside for what she'd done to me. I paid them whenever I praised her to others when I really wanted to slice away at her reputation. Those were the payments but she never knew them. However, I never knew her payments, but

I know she made them. I could tell."

And now the unthinkable: not only to forgive but seek the good. Nature abhors a vacuum and Jesus admits of no middle ground between hate and love. Pray for the one who sinned against you.

When you were a child you thought like a child, that pain was something to flee. Now in the adulthood of faith, suck up your hundred denarii, because someone took your ten thousand talents upon Himself (Matthew 18), and like a lamb led to slaughter and a sheep before its shearers was silent (Isaiah 53:7). He did not retaliate but "continued entrusting Himself to Him who judges justly" (1 Peter 2:23). Be so awash in the ocean of His love, my soul, that the shortcomings of all human loves will, more and more, seem but a trifling thing.

PLUCKED OUT OF THE BURNING

There is a professor I know who doesn't do small talk. Not on principle, mind you, but the man just can't. Now we all know that small talk is necessary, a lubricant to social intercourse, the wedge into profounder subjects from the opening "hello." But the doctor's conversations snap shut like a clamp, because when he's said all he has to say, it doesn't occur to him to stay longer. And I am here to testify that I have learned more about Scripture and humility from this person than from any man alive.

There is a woman I know who can't "do" crowds. We all say this, but she really can't. To enter a roomful of people on a Sunday morning is almost more than she can manage. To pray aloud at Saturday prayer meeting is not even thinkable, though her attendance is as good as a promise. Some day the Lord, in His mercy, may give a breakthrough, but it's been decades like this. And did I mention that in the Sunday school class she's taught for 20 years, enthralled 4-year-olds who are elsewhere rambunctious sit in a circle and have learned what to do with little hands and feet, and that Jesus died to take away their sins?

I have a friend who is helpless before a chocolate éclair. I'm talking about lifelong warfare, a waxing and waning of the battle manifest in shrinking and expanding girth. We're hoping that the latest victory is a final rout, though we have been this way before. And may I add that she is unequal in friendship and counsel, and has more than once laid down her life for me.

In 1751 there was a man who took himself to wife, and thereupon announced to the new Mrs. John Wesley that he was not willing to preach one sermon less in a married state than in a single one—embracing in a most literal sense Paul's counsel that "those who have wives should live as if they had none." His letters to his wife feel like acid splashed in the face (one critic called Wesley "granite in aspic"). And yet the man saved millions, a veritable Johnny Appleseed of church growth. Where Presbyterians sowed culture, his circuit riders sowed gospel—and with his brother Charles he left us some of the greatest hymns of the faith.

A century later came Charles Spurgeon, Spirit-filled preacher, man of prayer, founder of a college and orphanage, author of commentaries, propagator of uplifting literature, defender of godly biblical exegesis—and so encumbered by a melancholy spirit that he himself declared that "there are dungeons beneath the Castle of Despair," and that he had often been in them.

Firebrand preachers and lackluster husbands. Men of both prayer and clinical morbidity. Women of wisdom given to gluttony. Samson making shipwreck of his life but taking the prophets of Dagon down with him. How do you tally the sum of this? Where do you put the coordinating conjunction? "Wesley was a great soul winner, but he sure was a lousy husband!" or, "Wesley was a lousy husband, but what a soul winner!"

In 1753, Mr. Wesley, in the grip of serious illness, and "not knowing how it might please God to dispose of me," penned his own epitaph, which begins: "Here lies the body of John Wesley, A brand plucked out of the burning." Better words were never writ.

A 16-year-old boy I care deeply about is growing up with half a complement of parents, and the one who remains is obtuse in sports and tends to depression. Such are the children of the kingdom of God—all missing arms or limbs, all cracked vessels.

His mother doesn't always hear her children because she's lost in thought about some essay or other for a Christian magazine. Out of such raw material God is pleased to build His kingdom, the better to show the power is from Him.

The Lord will judge. And when He does (on that Day when no flesh shall boast), I know His weights and measures will be fair, and tempered with a better love than mine, and that the Wisdom who was by His side when He established earth and sky will cast His judgment in our favor.

OUT OF THE BLUE

The person who is depressed doesn't need a doctor's note to certify it's clinical. We're talking about a state of paralysis, fatigue, critically low energy reserves, and flirting with the fantasy of one's annihilation. Those are the body's own internal certifications.

The nondepressed don't go scot-free. Physical and spiritual wellness have their own dangers: smug disdain ("In the thought of one who is at ease there is contempt for misfortune," Job 12:5) and breach of the benefit-of-the-doubt principle ("love believes all things," 1 Corinthians 13:7). Let the happy be humble and remember: "Who knows a person's thoughts except the spirit of that person?" (1 Corinthians 2:11).

But what follows is addressed to the melancholy. Chipper readers will be voyeurs here.

First, pray, pray, pray. "Is anyone among you suffering? Let him pray. Is anyone cheerful? Let him sing praise" (James 5:13). Crying out "in supplications and prayers night and day" (1 Timothy 5:5) isn't just for widows. Anytime anyone says, "we were so utterly burdened beyond our strength that we despaired of life itself," we should recognize that the burden "was to make us rely not on ourselves but on God who raises the dead" (2 Corinthians 1:8-9). Repeat: He raises the dead.

Secondly, sort out sinful from non-sinful causes. How's your diet? How's your sleep life? Is there a chemical imbalance? I have had depression that a good night's rest cured. Figure out how much of your depression you come by honestly and how much is from attitude or behavior prohibited in the Bible. You don't rebuke a feeling of fatigue, but you rebuke a feeling of worthlessness, or envy, or fear of man.

On meds: Don't jump too quickly to medicate melancholia that might make you a more compassionate neighbor ("God . . . comforts us in all our affliction, so that we may be able to comfort those who are in any affliction" [2 Corinthians 1:3-4]). And grapple long and hard before you trade away the next Picasso "blue period" for a little Prozac peace of mind.

Mind your goals. If being rid of melancholy is your non-negotiable supplication, soul searching is in order to see if you haven't substituted a set of your own "virtues" for God's. What God highly prizes is prayer, faith, and endurance. To practice these is not just the means to the better Christian life; it is the better Christian life. Have you fixated on success, worldly approval, and independence from the need of daily grace, and made the disciplines of godliness mere steppingstones to them?

Depression calls for clear-minded thinking. I realize this is precisely the commodity you believe you can't muster, but you must. Depression thrives in foggy mental states like salmonella in a petri dish. I used to think I had to roll over when a depression came, at its first fluttering in the mind. Not so. You can talk to a depression, rebuke it. Rehearse the basics—you are a son or daughter, mightily loved by your Father.

Mentally separate out God's sovereignty from your responsibility: You are called to be faithful, not healthy. Make a list of what you can do right now: a load of ironing, clean out one kitchen drawer, prepare dinner. The beast will put up a fight, but it will not be your master.

If this can tide you over for an afternoon, you will be interested to find that the most acute depression (like the most acute emotion of being in love) cannot be sustained over the long haul. Afterwards, you will have only to deal with your baseline manageable melancholia. And at this stage, you might realize that depression is best handled by plunging in and helping others. Live as though you're not depressed (1 Corinthians 7:29-31).

The happy discovery is that even when depressed, you can be controlled by the Spirit and not the depression. You can have a moment-by-moment dependency on the Lover of your soul. You can say, "I'm depressed. So what?"—and carry on with the energy God supplies. All the while you keep in mind that your one neighbor has chronic back pain and your other neighbor has neurofibromatosis. You are not a tragic special case, cut off by a chasm from the rest of humanity. The condition is just what is common to man, the prescription is still faith, and the grace for it is inexhaustible.

MESSY IN THE MIDDLE

Pasteur Jean-Christophe Bieselaar is overworked and understaffed in Paris, for the glory of God. His email contained news of vandalism to his church, L'Eglise Protestante Evangelique de la Défense, and concluded with this note: "Let me tell you the truth as a pastor, can I? This is bad—and discouraging."

But that is the middle of a story, not an ending.

Pamela, a distant acquaintance, shared the dark night of her soul at a meeting in 1998: Her father was leaving her mother for a woman younger than his daughter. Devastation. Sackcloth and ashes. End of the world as Pamela knew it.

That was also the middle of the story. When I met her over breakfast recently she was radiant. She had seen over nine years that the Lord brings about the most improbably wonderful finales: the restoration of a family to more glory than before the tragedy. No wonder Abraham's son was named "laughter." Back in '98, Pam would have changed the hand dealt her. But, as a retreat speaker once said, "Would you really want to be in control of your own life? I can't even reset the clock on my VCR."

The end of a matter is what counts (Ecclesiastes 7:8). If the end is nice, the middle mess is not only bearable but takes on the endpoint's sheen. "Not only this valley but all this earthly past will have been Heaven to those who are saved. . . . This is what mortals misunderstand. They say of some temporal suffering, 'No future bliss can make up for it,' not knowing that Heaven, once attained, will work backwards and turn even that agony into a glory" (C.S. Lewis, *The Great Divorce*).

Satan wants you to believe the middle will last forever. A bit of the blues comes your way and you say, "Life stinks"—which is quite an extrapolation. But remember, the Polaroid shot of a tossed ball snapped at its arc's midpoint only seems to be stuck in the air. It won't stay there. The woman with the 12 years of bleeding (Luke 8) and the man lame for 38 years (John 5)—these are stories short in the reading but long in the living. But see what Jesus brought about.

Someone I love is presently perplexed that the Lord seemed to "dangle" a blessing in his life, only to snatch it away. "Why would God get my hopes up to let me down?" The short answer is "I don't know." The longer answer, from three decades' extra perspective, is that God, like any good Father, sees around corners for His children and snatches them out of the way of oncoming cars. He also drags His kids, kicking and screaming, from their cherished mud puddles, to take them to the beach.

Job, stuck in a brutal middle, cried, "I know that my Redeemer lives" (19:25). And that is the key to everything, to surviving brutal middles. "This is the victory that overcomes the world—our faith" (1 John 5:4). Those who believe not merely survive but flourish: "As they go through the Valley of Baca they make it a place of springs" (Psalm 84:6).

My brother Marc, in *God Still Loves the French*, chronicles 20 years of beating his head against the wall as a missionary in France. I don't know, does God still love the French? Does he love Pasteur Jean-Christophe Bieselaar? Bieselaar and Mailloux in France are not unlike Paul in Asia, whose life was messy in the middle freeze frames.

And so are we all "afflicted in every way, but not crushed; perplexed but not driven to despair" (2 Corinthians 4:8). A cloud of witnesses flanks the path of suffering, each one a living spring (Isaiah 32:2), dispensing ablutions of inspiration like so many cheering fans thrusting water cups along the Tour de France.

SECURITY COUNSEL

After breathing, food, water, sex, and sleep, what I need most to be a functioning person is security, according to psychologist Abraham Maslow. But Maslow died in 1970, and my God lives, and is presently challenging this notion in me, the better to show that man does not live by bread alone but by every word that proceedeth from His mouth.

"Job" is perhaps the commonest prefix to the word "security," and it is the kind I lack at the moment, having been plunged by Providence into unemployment and its handmaid, uncertainty.

Oswald Chambers, sounding like he's familiar with job loss, writes this about uncertainty: "Naturally, we are inclined to be so mathematical and calculating that we look upon uncertainty as a bad thing. We imagine that we have to reach some end, but that is not the nature of spiritual life. The nature of spiritual life is that we are certain in our uncertainty" (*My Utmost for His Highest*).

"Certain in our uncertainty." What does that mean? It means I missed the point if I've been living like my highest good is to be "set." "Even biology tells us that a high degree of habitual well-being is not advantageous to a living organism," Aleksandr Solzhenitsyn told the 1978 Harvard graduating class. I am presently reckoning with some of that disadvantageousness, and not enjoying it thus far.

Here is my postcard from the other side of the great gulf of gainful employment: The view is that in normal times one tends to derive one's security from notoriously losable things, even while continuing to believe one has placed one's house squarely on the Rock. If you are a child of His, God will not let that state of affairs persist indefinitely.

Dietrich Bonhoeffer writes in *The Cost of Discipleship*, "The disciple is dragged out of his relative security into a life of absolute insecurity (that is, in truth, into the absolute security and safety of the fellowship of Jesus); from a life which is observable and calculable (it is, in fact, quite incalculable) into a life where everything is unobservable and fortuitous (that is, into one which is necessary and calculable);

out of the realm of finite (which is in truth the infinite) into the realm of infinite possibilities (which is the one liberating reality)."

In children's terms, this translates as, "Shall we not take the adventure that Aslan hands us?" The nursery version lacks nothing of the profundity of the erudite quote. It communicates that in following Jesus we are following a Person, not a program, and must buckle up for all the quirkiness and unpredictability this entails. Chambers writes, "'Believe also in Me,' said Jesus, not 'Believe certain things about Me.'" (Note the fun corollaries of "breathless expectation" and "surprises all the time.")

It is in no other place than on this scary adventure that we learn to trust Jesus. How could it be otherwise? Commenting on Mark 2:14 (in which Levi the tax collector loses his job), Bonhoeffer writes, "Had Levi stayed at his post, Jesus might have been his present help in trouble, but not the Lord of his whole life. In other words, Levi would never have learned to believe. The new situation must be created, in which it is possible to believe in Jesus as God incarnate; that is, the impossible situation in which everything is staked solely on the word of Jesus."

One of life's joys is when the Lord quickens a

verse that long lay on the page inert. And when the epiphany is timely it is twice blest. I have derived encouragement of late from seven words I'd skimmed a hundred times unprofitably. The author of Hebrews, trying to sell us on Jesus as a flesh-and blood brother in our suffering, and not some unmoved Mover, cites three prophecies, of which the second is, "I will put My trust in Him" (2:13).

This is Jesus speaking of the Father. One can feel the pain of every slight and setback that could make the very Son of God feel faint. The background is not Constable but Bosch. The vow is likely made not once but every day, and many times a day. He looks up to the Father, Whose word is more security than the securities that all the world affords.

RESPECT THE EMOTIONS

I'm happy tonight. I don't imagine I've pronounced those three words together except once or twice in my life. I've got a praise song on, Martha Munizzi. I keep hitting replay. Here we go, ready? "Get to dancing, singing, jumping, leaping. Get to shouting, make it louder, make it glorious. Start rejoicing, praising, lifting, raising. Get to shouting, make it louder, make His praise glorious."

I remember a Korean woman telling me that in her culture people don't give themselves over to happiness—neither to sadness—because tomorrow both will pass. I guess that's right. Homeostasis. But this isn't tomorrow, it's today.

Don't you just love Jesus? They wanted Him and the boys to fast per cultural norm, but He wasn't playin'. You can fast tomorrow when I'm gone. Today I'm here, we eat and drink. Respect the wineskins.

Respect the emotions.

If the Lord told me to play a dirge tonight, I would do it, because He said so. But He doesn't, and He wouldn't. He says, "Is anyone among you suffering? Let him pray. Is anyone cheerful? Let him sing praise" (James 5:13). I'm sure on balance I suffer more than I'm cheerful—and I pray a lot. But tonight I'm cheerful (laughably inadequate word) and it's Martha Munizzi time.

I walked Spider earlier and tried to pray but all that came out was, "Thank you, Jesus. Thank you, Jesus. Thank you, Jesus. Thank you, Jesus." OK, I also prayed, "Who and what am I, that I should find such favor with You? Surely You have not treated me as my sins deserve. Surely mercy triumphs over judgment." I think He didn't mind the departure from the prayer list.

Did I put on Martha Munizzi to enhance the emotional experience? You bet. Let's enhance the emotional experience. Lord of body, soul, spirit, and emotions, have Your way in me. Is this joy? Yes indeed. It's always there somewhere underneath the careworn thoughts, but tonight it's a moon ascending. Come on now, dance with me. Carpe diem. Tomorrow I may be sad again. "Rejoice with those who rejoice, weep with those who weep" (Romans 12:15).

God has been known to coach us when feelings

are out of sync with facts: "'This day is holy to the Lord your God; do not mourn or weep.' For all the people wept as they heard the words of the Law. . . . 'Go your way. Eat the fat and drink sweet wine and send portions to anyone who has nothing ready, for this day is holy to our Lord. And do not be grieved, for the joy of the Lord is your strength'" (Nehemiah 8:9-10).

I spend a fair amount of time trying to decide if life is more sad or more happy—Flora and Meriwether vying in the last scene to make Cinderella's ballgown pink or blue. But in the One Story of which all stories partake, it definitely ends in pink not blue:

"And I saw in the right hand of Him who sat on the throne a scroll written inside and on the back, sealed with seven seals. And I saw a strong angel proclaiming with a loud voice, 'Who is worthy to open the scroll and to break its seals?' And no one in heaven or on the earth or under the earth was able to open the scroll or to look into it, and I began to weep loudly. . . . And one of the elders said to me, 'Weep no more; behold, the Lion of the tribe of Judah, the Root of David, has conquered, so that He can open the scroll and its seven seals.' And between the throne and the four living creatures and among the elders I saw a Lamb standing, as though it had been slain. . . .

"And they sang a new song" (Revelation 5).

Maybe the song goes like this: "Get to dancing, singing, jumping, leaping; got to shouting, make it louder, make it glorious. Start rejoicing, praising, lifting, raising. Make His praise glorious."

Tomorrow, I might be back to Psalm 88, camped out in perplexity and frustration. I always have permission to bring something real to the Lord, the Respecter of emotions; no need to hide or pretend.

But I am happy tonight.

MIRACLE WORKER

"A miracle is something only God can do." Dayle blurted that out as a definition when I told her my little tale, and what Heidi had said about it.

Dayle is a teacher of 4-year-olds and appreciates profundity at the far side of simplicity.

The story I had shared with her goes like this: A close relationship in my life came to an end without acrimony. For three years I had imagined every conceivable future scenario for this whirlwind but the one God brought to pass. The smoke cleared, the heat subsided, and left in its wake a residue of warm mutual affection. "It is not flesh and blood" that accomplished this. There is nothing in either of our histories to account for it. Heidi, who knows as much of the story as anyone, and who always chooses words with care, looked thoughtfully to the ground and said, "It's a miracle."

What is a miracle? Like other words we use daily and have never looked up (define frustration or coy), we all have some hazy concept of miracle honed by a thousand informal encounters with the lexical item. Good place to start.

We now dust off Merriam-Webster's and compare its offerings to our anecdotal preconception. Miracle: (1) "an extraordinary event manifesting divine intervention in human affairs"; (2) "an extremely outstanding or unusual event, thing, or accomplishment."

Not bad, I think (definition No. 2 shows the movement away from a divine source, as well as the natural expanding boundaries of terms to include analogous phenomena). But you and I are people of the Book, and I don't mean the Collegiate Dictionary 10th edition. To the Law and the Prophets, then.

Where Webster's is a systematic text, the Bible is a book of vignettes about nomads, war, and real estate disputes. It is very low on definitions (try finding Trinity). We discover a few Hebrew and Greek words translated "miracle," "sign," "wonder," etc. The cumulative force of these in context suggests a homely definition of miracle as an unusual event that God brings about. Dayle's definition.

Now philosophers and theologians don't get

paid for simple definitions. They get paid to multiply distinctions. A few that have been suggested over the years are as follows:

David Hume (1711-1776) called miracles "a violation of natural law." But as theologian John Frame says, "violation is inappropriate, since this world belongs to God. It is no violation for Him to do as He wishes in His own creation" (*The Doctrine of God*). A less egregious variation on the "violation" idea (but liable to the same objection) is that of miracle as exception to or suspension of natural law.

Theologian B.B. Warfield tried to help by offering the distinction "extra-natural" rather than "contra-natural." Unfortunately, this is not radically different from Hume's supernatural agency acting contrary to "natural law."

The breakthrough comes when you realize that there is no such thing as "natural law" in the traditional sense. There are only the decrees of God. "In this sense," says Frame, "natural laws are never broken, and miracle should not be seen as any sort of exception to natural law." There exists no demigod-like mechanism between God and us that He winds up and lets loose. All God's actions are direct.

Theologian Vern Poythress puts it this way: "God

as the primary cause is active in bringing about all the events in the world, both ordinary events and extraordinary ones. But in the case of ordinary events He works in conjunction with secondary causes" (*Redeeming Science*). He cites Psalm 104:14 as an example, "You make the grass to grow for the livestock." The line between miracle and general providence is a blurry one, not a sharp one.

End of story. Two people who couldn't love their way out of a paper bag yet had this one thing going for them: They prayed through the whole nine yards of the relationship, surrendering their will to God's. And because "the Lord preserves the simple" (Psalm 116:6), He preserved them from harm and even brought about a surprising denouement—whether through psychological secondary causes or otherwise—that left them blessed and His grace glorified.

What is a miracle, then? I'm with Dayle: "A miracle is something only God can do."

COUNT IT ALL JOY

I am happy these days, because of a command. One is not supposed to be happy about commands. Commands are a superseding of the will. America was founded on the impulse against that. Why then does the Psalmist exclaim, "I will lift up my hands toward your commandments, which I love" (Psalm 119:48)? Imagine loving a commandment.

"Be joyful in hope" (Romans 12:12). The saying comes to resemble, in 21st-century fatigue, the equivalent of that other empty hortatory leave-taking, "Have a nice day." Yeah, right. Sure, sure.

In one sense the last three years of my life have been a search for joy. I don't think this is purely hedonism (although, praise God, John Piper has taken out the stigma with his insistence on "Christian hedonism"): What but my joy can make Jesus delectable and desirable to my neighbor?

Is it not our hard-won birthright? "You have loved righteousness and hated wickedness; therefore God, your God, has anointed you with the oil of gladness beyond your companions" (Hebrews 1:9).

I love that. Read around the verse and you will see the man Jesus—strong and sinewy, praying with loud cries and tears—who has made us a band of brothers and is not ashamed of it. He locks arms to praise His Father "in the midst of the congregation." He casts His lot with us forever and will not relinquish His human clothing for all eternity. The Divinity is now and henceforth human-divinity, or divine-humanity. One should be stoned for such a thing if it were not there in Hebrews.

But I stray. The joy. Who has known joy except for those rare "stabs" in childhood, the siren of a distant country that came over you at play, but only for a split second, and not so anyone would notice? Or less yet in adulthood, of that quickening while you're minding your own business: "almost like a heartbreak," "an unsatisfied desire which is itself more desirable than any other satisfaction" (C.S. Lewis, *Surprised by Joy*).

One grows up, accrues duties like barnacles, and becomes suspicious of the rumor of joy. "Be worthy of your beard," they used to say in the late Middle

Ages, that darkness before the dawn.

And yet joy is all over Scripture. A concordance will give you an idea of the importance of joy to God. (Should I not be obsessed by what obsesses God?) Of the fruit of the Spirit it comes second, after only "love," of which stuff God Himself is made.

But the Lord knows this about His child: I need to be commanded to rejoice or I won't. There are personal reasons for that: 1) Superstition—don't let yourself be happy or something bad will happen; jump before you're pushed; 2) You don't deserve to be joyful—it is presumptuous and unseemly. Your proper posture is to be abject in your utter sinfulness.

I lived so long in a pit that I thought it was my God-assigned home and I should be content. I was hanging draperies and inviting people in—mostly women. Some of them lived in the same kind of house, and we discussed our living quarters together over tea, and how many years we had lived there. We said how grateful we were that God loved us anyway—in spite of the fact that we were living totally defeated lives.

But what can I do if you command joy, Lord? If you give me permission, if you tell me I must—as if insisting I take this festive package with the bow on top—and that if I refuse, I am not being humble but disobedient and ungrateful? In that case, I say: "Aye-aye, Lord, I rejoice!" And, "not my feet only but also my hands and my head" (John 13:9).

Joy is no stranger anymore but comes to stay. It has as its content the "yes and amen" promises. It rooms with sorrow but I understand that's the deal, for now. And comes anon the "breakthrough" joy, the promissory of a distant land where joy is unalloyed with pain. The servant is not better than his master, after all—who offered supplications "with loud cries and tears," and thus received the "oil of gladness," rolling off His beard and unto us.

KEEPING IT REAL

"Be humble." Go ahead: On your mark, get set, go be humble. What? You're not concentrating; try harder! Make like a Stanislovsky actor and dredge up feelings of self-deprecation. Shoot for that low opinion of your talents that you're sure is the essence of humility. You may not get there, but the devil will be pleased enough by all the time you've spent thinking of yourself. Or you may indeed arrive at humility, and notice it—which saddles you with another problem: pride in your humility.

I recall only one moment of true humility in my life. A friend had come to see my newborn daughter 26 years ago, and I exclaimed, uncharacteristically, "Isn't she beautiful!" My friend replied with a polite chuckle something to the effect that I was humility-challenged. I can tell you, brothers, that it was years before I ever breathed another word of praise about a child of mine. The odd thing though—and the thing my visitor could not have known—is that she had caught me in a rare instance of total self-forgetfulness. Never have I been so free from pride or fear of man as in that exclamation. It was all God and wonder and nothing else.

My choice to marry was different. I married an Asian man, which prompted a friend to ask years later: "Were you thinking you were tough enough to take on the challenge of 2,000 years of Eastern Confucian treatment of women?" She was right except that it was not toughness but humility that I thought I possessed in quantities surpassing others of my gender. I was going to out-Korean the Korean women. I made lavish promises that now call to mind the effusiveness of Israel on the banks of Canaan: "Far be it from us that we should forsake the Lord to serve other gods!" Joshua, more sober, replied, "You are not able to serve the Lord" (Joshua 24:16,19).

Who ever became humble by being told to? More likely he was stunned by a series of reality checks. He arrived at the banquet and grabbed the best seat at the table and was summarily told by the lord of the banquet to slide down a few chairs because a person more distinguished had walked in (Luke 14:7-11).

Would you be free of the roller-coaster ride of a life of serial humiliations? Then assess yourself accurately. Humility is acknowledging reality, nothing more or less. And here are some realities: Everyone is smart at some things and stupid at some things. The Lord has apportioned gifts so that no one has all of them. Your opponent with the opposite millennial view has valid points that you should listen to because the Spirit lives in him, too. The difference in knowledge between you and your brother—as compared to God's knowledge—is like the difference between two boys on the Jersey shore boasting about who can throw a rock that reaches closest to England.

A former president of Westminster Seminary during a faculty meeting asked the meaning of a word he didn't know. After the meeting a professor asked him how he had admitted that bit of ignorance. The president replied thus: He had written his Ph.D. on the Olivet Discourse. By the time he was done, he supposed that he knew as much on the subject as any man alive. But he also realized that compared to what there is to know, he knew nothing. Since then, he was never unduly intimidated by knowledgeable people.

The apostle Paul makes us blush. He says unseemly things like, "You yourselves know how

I lived among you . . . , serving the Lord with all humility" (Acts 20:18-19). Either he is proud or he is eminently realistic: "What do you have that you did not receive?" (1 Corinthians 4:7). So devoid of illusions is he, so free from prejudice, even toward himself, that he can speak of his own humility without a hint of awkwardness. Nor is King David embarrassed to call himself great—because he is straight on the Source of it: "Your gentleness made me great" (2 Samuel 22:36). The eye fixed on Christ sees clearly, succumbing to neither pride nor inferiority, because it is not concerned with the self at all.

Humility. No need to foist a fiction on yourself: I am the chief of sinners. I am a daughter of the King.

WE SHALL HAVE SPRING AGAIN

Imagine that you have been cold for a very long time, as long as you can remember. You are in a snowy landscape, but this is not the pleasant kind of snow of a Thomas Kincade painting, where hot cocoa and biscuits beckon from a thatched cottage. This is the frigid, relentless white of a tundra, and you have been plying it for miles, passenger on a sledge commandeered by a white witch.

If there is a book in your house called *The Lion, the Witch and the Wardrobe*, you may read a longer version of this miserable journey from the start of chapter 11.

On the joyless ride is Edmund, a character whom Mr. Beaver said brought to mind the word treacherous the minute he laid eyes on him, but a character that you are feeling sorry for—in other words, someone like you and me. Edmund notices that he is feeling much less cold. Then he notices a curious and unaccustomed noise, a "strange, sweet, rustling, chattering noise" (don't you love the word "chattering" here?), which he identifies as the sound of running water: "bubbly, splashy, even (in the distance) roaring . . . a drip-drip-drip from the branches of all the trees."

We can pass over the rest about the more delicious sounds to come—of "chirruping" birds, first singly and then as of a whole forest awaking—because by now you know what's happening. The sledge is stalling and sticking, the witch is calling down oaths, and green patches of spongy spring grass are popping out all over.

Aslan is near, that's the reason. His breath warms the sin-cursed ground, thaws the icicles around relationships, and ends indentured servitude to the witch we loved for Turkish delight. A lifelong winter that was never Christmas melts into first Christmas.

Mr. Beaver breaks into his Magnificat:

"Wrong will be right, when Aslan comes in sight,
At the sound of his roar, sorrows will be no
more,
When he bares his teeth, winter meets its death,

And when he shakes his mane, we shall have
spring again."

But is this really true, or just a tale for children? (Like the jaded dwarfs, you refuse to be taken in.) Are sorrows truly no more after God's incarnation? Is your work really freed from futility and frustration? Are your relationships so sanctified? Have you seen an end to enslaving idols and cravings for Turkish delight? Or is this pie in the sky by and by?

Let us survey the evidences:

You're still short-tempered—but a couple of times last month you said you were sorry.

Your marriage has had its peaks and vales, but you are still together.

You sin every day, but you don't find it pleasant anymore; you're not blasé about it anymore. You want to change.

One thought in 10 in your head is a thought of gratitude—but that's way up from zero.

You recently wrecked a relationship, big time. But you went back and tried to make it right. Feebly, timidly, awkwardly. But in the old days you wouldn't have even done that.

The first thing on your mind when you wake up

in the morning is still "&*%$#, it's Monday." But at least the ninth or 10th thing on your mind nowadays is the goodness of God.

You used to spend 15 minutes obsessing to every one minute praying, but now the proportions are beginning to reverse.

As time goes by, the things of earth seem thinner and the things of heaven seem more concrete.

Sorrows abound, but comforts more abound. And these are less and less the comforts of escapism but those of reality—the soon and certain return of the King.

For Christ has come indeed. But you live in the in-between time, where old age and new age overlap, and things are messy. The Lion is come—yea, is sacrificed on the stone table—but the book has several chapters in it yet. This is a mop-up operation but not a chimera; the skirmishes are real. Let us seize the day and its power "until the day dawns and the morning star rises" with all the confidence of spring.

NOT THIS MORNING'S FAITH

Whoever wants to live Christianity that's not a sham must reckon with a little noted peculiarity about life: It is a dish served up one moment at a time. Failure to reckon sufficiently with this fact renders faith an abstraction, and there is no such thing as faith in the abstract. There is faith or there is sentimentality.

Angels do not have to contend with this particular wrinkle of reality. And apart from the grace of God, I wonder if they do not wonder how Mary could sing the Magnificat at one moment and in a successive moment fret that her Son has gone mad. They must wonder why Solomon, Mr. Wisdom, proceeded to make such unwise choices in marriage and horse breeders. They must tremble at this created thing called time when they see pastors—godly men for years—inexplicably fall into adultery.

Francis Schaeffer put it this way: "This morning's

faith will never do for this noon. The faith of this noon will never do for supper time. The faith of supper time will never do for the time of going to bed" (*True Spirituality*). Because life is a new thing every moment, faith must be new every moment too.

The faith we are talking about, of course, is the confidence that Jesus—the radiance of God's glory, the One for Whom and by Whom all things were created—made purification for your sins and then called you His brother and joint heir for the present age and ages to come. We said we believed that once. Have we, over time, come to treat the blood of Jesus like it's nothing more than "getting registered to vote or choosing our HMOs," as one woman I know put it? Are we bored?

Satan doesn't mind our faith as long as it stays in the voter registration category. The demon Screwtape tries to be sanguine on the disastrous occasion of one "patient's" conversion to Christianity: "The great thing is to prevent his doing anything. As long as he does not convert it into action, it does not matter how much he thinks about this new repentance."

It's partly the fault of that other created thing the angels are unsaddled with: these darned tents we live in. We're so tied to them. One day they're a hot red fire engine, and we think we soar spiritually. The next day they're cranky and creaky and they pull the soul right down with them. I just got a letter from a guy who's normally doing back-flips praising the Lord. In today's letter he writes, "I think I'm going through a dry spell." The fella thinks it's spiritual but it could be just a touch of flu.

There is an easy way to "test yourselves" and check "whether you are in the faith" (2 Corinthians 13:5) at any given moment: anxiety. I am talking about a handy self-diagnostic tool—a kind of spiritual breathalyzer—and I check myself several times a day. Most times I am dismayed to find an indictable anxiety level that tells me that, in this moment, I am not trusting in God's unfailing love, not believing the promises, not being aware of the practical present value of Christ's work for this very moment's struggles. I am stumbling around in defeat and fear because I have lapsed once again into lies.

My friend David calls these emotional gauges "red flags" and "green flags"—the red ones, a nagging discomfort alerting you to slippage in trust; the green ones, a peaceful disposition of heart that accompanies pinpoint present walking in the truth, even in the midst of daunting outward circumstances.

The Apostle goes on to counsel the Corinthians, "Or do you not realize this about yourselves, that Jesus Christ is in you?" Realize it, my soul, dagnabit! Good Lord, why does it slip away a thousand times a day, and always present itself to me again as something new?

How about we start immediately? Drop whatever you're doing and take inventory. What's the dull pebble in your shoe this very second? Anxiety? Fear? Covetousness? Panic? Chase down the source. What exactly are you afraid of? Shall we pray: Lord, forgive us. Give us grace that we may trust in You this moment, that we may reign with You right now.

NONE OF MY BUSINESS

I like *Star Trek* best when it's most like *The Twilight Zone*. A 1967 episode titled "The City on the Edge of Forever" raises the tantalizing question of what it would be like if you could go back and edit your personal history. We've all been there.

On Stardate 3134.0 the *Enterprise* discovers a planet on which stands a free-standing door leading to any time or place. In pursuit of a renegade member of their crew, Capt. James T. Kirk and Mr. Spock leap over the threshold into Depression-era Manhattan, and the spaceship disappears because it no longer exists (you get the idea).

Ducking a cop after stealing clothes off a fire escape to conceal Spock's attention-grabbing ears, the two disappear into a basement, where they meet a young, idealistic social worker named Edith Keeler, who works for the 21st Street Mission and shows them kindness. Kirk begins to fall in love.

Spock, being Spock, is otherwise occupied analyzing data from his tricorder to learn what parts of history have been altered by the party's intrusion into the suddenly unfrozen past. The information is appalling. Edith is soon to be struck and killed by a car. But wait! The time interlopers' visit will somehow save the lovely social worker from that fate. Praise the Lord!

Praise the Lord? Just one problem. Her life now extended, Ms. Keeler will go on to lead a pacifist movement so successful that it delays the United States' entry into World War II enough to allow the Nazis to achieve their goal of world domination.

Now, let's beam back to planet Earth's real history: In 1937, on the eve of world war, an expulsion of missionaries from southern Ethiopia left 75 new converts to fend for themselves. Returning after the war, the gospel workers found the faith had spread like wildfire, more than if they had been allowed to remain in the country.

And now, my own story: I have been asking, seeking, knocking at the throne of grace for 17 months for simple, sweet sleep. Function is impaired by day, and thoughts assail by night. Meanwhile, my friend Kyung phoned to report excitedly a dramatic deliverance from depression three weeks ago.

Why not me? On the beach at Tiberias, Jesus has just divulged to Simon the gruesome manner of his death. The apostle casts a glance over his shoulder to John and asks (as I ask about Kyung), "Lord, what about him?" The Lord replies, effectively, that this is none of Peter's business.

There are things revealed, and there are secret things (Deuteronomy 29:29). Among the things revealed is that I should continue to "pray and not lose heart" (Luke 18:1). Among the things hidden are the hypothetical imponderables of regular good nights of sleep.

What are the blessings of sleeplessness? I might not have learned to pray militantly. I might not have had to dig deeper for the water table of faith. I might have confused my natural strength for His supernatural strength. When God says no, what does He foresee down the road that I do not? What if He had answered prayers to keep the missionaries in Ethiopia in 1937?

What if God is longing to answer your prayer and just waiting for the right time? There would be precedents:

"For a long time I have held My peace; I have kept still and restrained Myself; now I will cry out like a woman in labor. . . . I will lay waste mountains and hills, . . . I will lead the blind in a way that they do not know, . . . I will turn the darkness before them into light. . . . These are the things I do, and I do not forsake them" (Isaiah 42:14-16).

"God is represented as treasuring the prayers of His saints in vials. . . . They are placed like fragrant flowers in the chambers of the king. . . . And later they are represented as poured out upon the earth; and lo, there are voices, and thunderings, and great providential movements fulfilling God's purposes for His kingdom. We are called 'The Lord's remembrances.' And are commanded to give Him no rest, day or night, but to crowd the heavens with our petitions. And in due time the answer will come with its accumulated blessings. No breath of prayer is lost. The longer it waits, the larger it becomes" (A.B. Simpson).

SHARING THE FREIGHT

My brother confessed to his friend Hugh sweaty palms over the prospect of marriage: "I'm not sure I could live with her on a desert island." Hugh replied, "Guess what, you're not going to live with her on a desert island." That was 1979 and Marc and Aline were married and have one of the best marriages I know.

Such married-couple households are finally in a minority, according to the 2006 American Community Survey published by the Census Bureau. The panic this news may produce in Christian circles tends to a knee-jerk redoubling of our efforts to make marriage tighter, more intimate. More intimate is a good thing, but more exclusive may not be, writes Stephanie Coontz in an op-ed piece for *The New York Times*.

Coontz says "it has only been in the last century that Americans have put all their emotional eggs in the basket of coupled love." What's the problem, you ask? The problem is the unintended collateral damage that "we have also neglected our other relationships, placing too many burdens on a fragile institution and making social life poorer in the process."

If Coontz's contention strikes you as evangelical heresy, the strains of warning about excessive freight on the marriage relationship do find echoes among the brethren. Francis Schaeffer wrote in 1971 in *True Spirituality*: "No love affair between a man and a woman has ever been great enough to hang everything on. It will crumble away under your feet. And as the edges begin to break away the relationship is destroyed."

Likewise, a lament for the underappreciation of non-marital friendships is sounded by C.S. Lewis in *The Four Loves*: "Very few modern people think Friendship a love of comparable value or even a love at all. . . . To the Ancients, Friendship seemed the happiest and most fully human of all loves. . . . The modern world, in comparison, ignores it."

The correlative demise of friendship and unrealistic exaltation of marriage as the source of emotional sustenance is traced by both Coontz and Lewis in complementary lines. Coontz hypothesizes as follows: "By the early 20th century . . . the sea change in the culture wrought by the industrial economy had loosened social obligations to neighbors and kin, giving rise to the idea that individuals could meet their deepest needs only through romantic love, culminating in marriage . . . it's the expansion of the post-industrial economy that seems to be driving us back to a new dependence on marriage . . . work has devoured time once spent cultivating friendships."

Lewis offers his own hypothesis. In almost reminiscing tones about a social matrix gone the way of Oldowan tools in the West, he writes: "Long before history began we men have got together apart from the women and done things. We had to. . . . We not only had to do the things, we had to talk about them. We had to plan the hunt and the battle. When they were over we had to hold a post mortem and draw conclusions for future use. We liked this even better."

He continues: "Those are the golden sessions; when four or five of us after a hard day's walking have come to our inn; when our slippers are on, our feet spread out toward the blaze and our drinks at our elbows; when the whole world, and something beyond the world, opens itself to our minds as we talk. . . . Life—natural life—has no better gift to give.

Who could have deserved it?"

From the sublime to the less sublimc thc cult holiday movie *White Christmas* features Rosemary Clooney and Vera-Ellen setting straight their boyfriends (and each other) in song about their limitations: "Lord help the mister who comes between me and my sister. And Lord help the sister who comes between me and my man."

The book of Hebrews' recipe for spiritual health is to not forsake congregating together, and to "exhort one another every day" (Hebrews 3:13), implying a larger company than a duo. Speaking personally, I have had a marriage and I have had friendships. What I have found is that, even for the sake of the marriage, it is best not to live with a spouse on a desert island.

FROM MANY NATIONS, ONE BODY

Ilya Lizorkin had to shift gears. He started a worship service for Russian Jews, and Muslims showed up. Of course, he didn't start the thing at all but Jesus did, and His Spirit blows where it wills. Men of understanding let it blow and step out of the way.

I came to learn about the Rock of Israel congregation (don't call it a church) while looking for something positive in the early weeks of last summer's Israeli-Lebanese troubles. I happened to run into Fred Klett at the post office and vaguely knew of his founding of CHAIM, a Christian ministry camped out in promises to bring the Jews back in the last days: "And even they, if they do not continue in their unbelief, will be grafted in, for God has power to graft them in again" (Romans 11:23).

Fred explained that he had met Marko Malyj, son of Ukrainian immigrants, at the Lausanne Consultation on Jewish Evangelism. Add another Soviet Jewish immigrant with a Muslim father, and a Bible study taught in Russian and English was formed. (Did you know that the Philadelphia area has 100,000 Russian speakers, most of whom don't know their right hand from their left spiritually? Fifty thousand of these are Russian Jews, the rich silt of three waves of immigration—the last in 1992—prompted by tyranny and economic poverty in the faltering Soviet Union.)

A providential encounter with two influential Russian Jewish women in the community resulted in another group, and soon there were several cells—and the dawning recognition that it was about time for a bona fide congregation. Fred and Marko heard about Ilya Lizorkin at Reformed Theological Seminary in Florida and "began working on getting Ilya to come to Philadelphia."

Ilya invited me to his office. I asked how he became a Christian and he said, "I wouldn't put it that way. I became a follower of the Messiah." He likes to call himself a Messianic Jew or a Jewish Christian, and I duly noted the semantic preference. It was my first hint at a cultural-religious sensitivity that has been crucial to the success of the mission of reaching out to Jewish and Muslim transplants.

Ilya's own spiritual odyssey illustrates this. Born in Samarkand, the fourth-holiest city of Islam, he spent his first years in Odessa, Ukraine, moved to Tajikistan at age 8, and then returned to Ukraine to pursue nursing. He became a believer through Jews for Jesus on the streets of Odessa in the wake of perestroika, a de-regionalized limbo and religious vacuum left by the implosion of the Soviet Union. Ilya tells me that Russian Jews felt culturally Jewish but not religiously Jewish at the time. And so, though ironic to American ears, Jews for Jesus actually offered disaffected religious nomads like Ilya more Jewishness.

This historic peculiarity explains the surprising twist in the Rock of Israel founding. Ilya was fishing for Russian Jews and netted a family from Kyrgyzstan, a former Soviet republic that is nominally Muslim. He discovered the family was no more religiously Muslim than Ilya had been religiously Jewish. One Tajikistan woman (who during worship follows the Muslim practice of rubbing the blessing into her face), when asked about her attendance at Rock of Israel, replied that she comes "because my countryman runs it."

Rock of Israel obliges by including on its liturgical calendar not only Jewish holidays but Muslim nonreligious holidays like Norooz, a spring equinox celebration from which Ilya preaches the Resurrection. I worshipped with Rock of Israel on two Saturday evenings, and we opened with "the Sh'ma" from Deuteronomy 6: "Hear, O Israel: The Lord our God, the Lord is one . . ." (but in Hebrew).

I got to hear Andrei from Odessa on electric bass. I broke bread with a nice Jewish girl from Brooklyn named Lauren at the home of her Kyrgyzstan friends Ulan and Mira, whom she led to the Lord—after her own conversion by a cabby in New York. Our being all together reminded me somehow of the wall hanging I had spotted in Ilya's office:

"The wolf shall dwell with the lamb, and the leopard shall lie down with the young goat, and the calf and the lion and the fattened calf together; and a little child shall lead them" (Isaiah 11:6).

HE CAME AS A FLOOD

God hides nuggets of gold in plain day and surprises us with new findings in passages we've read a hundred times. I came across this yesterday:

"Now those who were scattered because of the persecution that arose over Stephen traveled as far as Phoenicia and Cyprus and Antioch, speaking the word to no one except Jews. But there were some of them, men of Cyprus and Cyrene, who on coming to Antioch spoke to the Hellenists also, preaching the Lord Jesus. And the hand of the Lord was with them, and a great number who believed turned to the Lord. The report of this came to the ears of the church in Jerusalem, and they sent Barnabas to Antioch. When he came and saw the grace of God, he was glad and he exhorted them all to remain faithful to the Lord with steadfast purpose, for he was a good man, full of the Holy Spirit and of faith" (Acts 11:19-24).

Antioch means nothing to you. It's a smudge buried in a middle chapter, a name on a list. You read "Jerusalem" and "Antioch" in one breath and conjure cities of equal nebulousness. They are in fact Plainview, Texas, and Chicago for size difference. I learned that "Antioch on the Orontes" (present day Antakya, Turkey) was the third-largest metropolis in the empire, after Rome and Alexandria. Picture all the best and all the worst of great cities: megalomaniac building projects of Pompeii, Julius Caesar, Herod the Great, Augustus, Tiberius, crime, theaters, squalor, aqueducts, shrine prostitution, public baths, fountains, amphitheaters, paved street with colonnade, crossroads of continents, and three major trade routes.

Who founded the church at Jerusalem? The Apostles (for human proxy). Who founded the church at Antioch? Unknown and unnamed refugees from Cyrene and Cyprus. How did it happen? "The hand of the Lord was with them" (v. 21). What was the response of the church leaders who got wind of this irregular development 300 miles away? They sent Barnabas to check it out. What did Barnabas do? He came, he saw, he got out of the way of the Holy Spirit.

"The wind blows where it wishes," and even Jesus

gave the Spirit wide berth when the disciples came to Him with complaint: "'Teacher, we saw someone casting out demons in Your name, and we tried to stop him, because he was not following us.' But Jesus said, 'Do not stop him'" (Mark 9:38-39). Moses was not so foolhardy as to halt a Holy Ghost locomotive when his disciples brought complaint about two men prophesying outside the normal top-down sanctioned church structures: "Joshua the son of Nun, the assistant of Moses from his youth, said, 'My lord Moses, stop them.' But Moses said to him, 'Are you jealous for my sake? Would that all the Lord's people were prophets, that the Lord would put His Spirit on them!'" (Numbers 11:28-29).

Details on the Antioch phenomenon are not given—except they prayed and fasted (Acts 13:1-3). Wouldn't you love to know how it happened—no formal church building, no sound system, no seminarians, no website, no Power Point, no minivan? But Antioch became the launch pad for Paul's and Barnabas's missionary adventures. By the time of Theodosius, there were 100,000 believers.

Do you think it was anything like the Welsh revival of 1904, where a teenager named Florrie Evans publicly declared in a youth meeting that she loved Jesus with all her heart, and the Spirit fell and ignited Cardiganshire?

Was it like the Korean Pentecost of 1907? Missionaries William Blair and Bruce Hunt explained, "We had reached a place where we dared not go forward without God's presence. Very earnestly we poured out our hearts before Him, searching our hearts and seeking to meet the conditions. God heard us and gave us an earnest that week of what was to come. Before the meetings closed, the Spirit showed us plainly that the way of victory for us would be a way of confession, of broken hearts, and bitter tears." Missionary Jonathan Goforth adds, "They honored God the Holy Spirit by six months of prayer and then He came as a flood."

"Let your fleece lie on the threshing floor of supplication till it's wet with the dew of heaven" (C. H. Spurgeon).

BEYOND HUMAN CONTROL

The strange doings of canaries and coalmines are not to be compared to those of tram-harnessed, blind horses in those ore-veined hills of Wales from 1904 to 1906. It was a scene like Babel, but between man and equus rather than man and man. To put it delicately, miners suddenly stopped talking like miners. And their horses, no longer able to understand the colliers' commands, lowered their ears and dug in their hooves. Coal production fell off around the country.

That's not all. Businesses went into foreclosure—pubs and taverns, to be precise. Emergency meetings of local councils were called to discuss what was to be done with the police force since the police had so little to do. Nightly prayer meetings multiplied like spores from Amlwch to Llanerchymedd to Disgwylfa.

They say you should watch what you pray for. As the century turned a page, churches around the world were praying for revival—from Moody Bible Institute, to the Keswick Convention in England, to Wansan in Korea, to 10,000-strong prayer circles in Melbourne. The Methodists in the United States raised $20 million for programs to win 2 million souls. Historian J. Edwin Orr relates with amusement one Methodist's later confession: "God waited till we got our project out of the way before He sent revival."

Wales is the land of silver-tongued orators. But it was none of these, nor committee programs, that lit the fuse. That came in February 1904 in a weekly youth group meeting in New Quay, Cardigan, when pastor Joseph Jenkins asked: "What does Jesus mean to you?" Silence. Then young Florrie Evans declared simply, "I love Jesus with all my heart." The youth group ignited. A visiting evangelist named Seth Joshua tried to close worship services, but they "went on beyond human control." He would close with the benediction, and in a moment, somebody would start praying again.

A 26-year-old coal miner named Evan Roberts, enrolled in ministerial studies at the Presbyterian Newcastle Emlyn, got wind of this and was electrified; he had been praying for revival for 11 years. Roberts and other students asked the principal to suspend classes for a week so they could attend Seth Joshua's week of meetings in Blaenanerch. Principal Phillips wisely consented. When the week was up, Roberts couldn't concentrate on his studies; he kept hearing a voice calling him home to preach to his hometown youth. He asked Phillips what he should do. Said the school head, "The devil never gives orders like that."

Roberts's parents were surprised to see their son on the doorstep, and more surprised when he said he had come back to preach to the youth of Loughor. "We were in church on Sunday and the pastor didn't announce it," they said. "The pastor doesn't know yet," young Evan said.

The pastor gave him the subprime slot, Monday night. But after Monday folks asked for more, and he ended up staying the week. His message was simple: Confess any known sin to God; put away any doubtful habit; obey the Spirit promptly; confess Christ publicly.

Grocery stores emptied, shopkeepers hung their "closed" signs early, miners and steelworkers, emerging from darkened shafts, scrubbed, and donned their Sunday finest for church. What they found was some preaching but mostly prayer and testimony. One hundred thousand were added to the church rolls. (A revival cynic later noted that after five years, 25,000 people had left the church. But which 25,000? Revival converts, or original members who couldn't stand the light?)

The revival never became a cult of Evan Roberts. He wouldn't let it, refusing even to announce where he would show up next. Nor must you imagine thousands assembled in packed auditoriums; it was, rather, a thousand points of light at local churches.

If you had been in Wales before Florrie Evans stood up in youth group in February 1904, you would have said this was a country, if ever there was one, that didn't need revival. The churches were orthodox, pulpit oration was never better, and the youth groups were full of decent, God-fearing Welsh kids. Makes you wonder what it is God wants from us.

USELESSNESS OF DELIGHT

My mother has always been surprised that I have good childhood memories of my father. He was almost never home, whereas she was home all the time. The exception was Sunday mornings, when after Mass he drove us to Lamoureaux Field for batting and fielding practice. No one had to tell him to: We played baseball on Sunday because it was a blast—for him. And it was always capped off with a visit to Beaudette's Apothecary for coffee "cabinets" (Rhode Island for milkshake) and nabs (Nabisco peanut butter crackers) on the high swivel stools at the bar. I don't remember that kind of detail in most of the rest of my life.

It raises the question of what it is to be a parent in loco parentis for our own heavenly Father. We usually think of proper Bible study as working in the direction from the Bible to life (Normative to

Situational), but in the investigation at hand, moving from life to Bible proves as instructive. I consider those Sunday mornings, I weigh my mother's mathematical premises and conclusion, I note a counterintuitive outcome, and I ask the Scriptures to make sense of it. That is, did my father, for all his mistakes (and James 3:2 says we all make them), stumble on biblical gold unawares? And if so, O Lord, show me now that I may at least finish well.

The teaching was at once too subtle and too obvious, the weave of my net at once too tight and too loose to catch the thing. Feed, shelter, protect, train were the mandates I has taken from Holy Writ, and as a mother did better in some areas than others. These were more or less empirical and quantifiable, duties that could be discharged without the heart engaged, like a well-trained monkey.

But what was too huge to be seen was the eternal love Triangle, three Persons savoring each other's company long before "the morning stars sang together and all the sons of God shouted for joy " (Job 38:7), a mutual delight that formed the matrix of the universe. Delight was before anything.

What was too small to be seen was the dropped hints that were never commands but not the less incumbent: "The Lord your God is in your midst, a mighty One who will save; He will rejoice over you with gladness" (Zephaniah 3:17). "He brought me out into a broad place; He rescued me, because He delighted in me" (Psalm 18:19); "For the Lord takes pleasure in His people " (Psalm 149:4). "You shall be a crown of beauty in the hand of the Lord, and a royal diadem in the hand of your God. You shall no more be termed Forsaken, and your land shall no more be termed Desolate, but you shall be called My Delight is in Her" (Isaiah 62:3-4).

Delight is the most useless of things. It doesn't get the house clean or the bills paid. Useless—like rainbows. Like Beethoven's Ninth.

Delight covers a multitude of parenting shortcomings. You may be too strict or too lenient and still come out all right, if you delight in your children. They will know it, for delight cannot be hidden. It finds excuse to ooze all over the place. It seeks a getaway vacation with the beloved when it's not convenient. It asks different questions than duty. Duty says, "I should." Delight says, "I want to." Duty is efficient. Delight tends to anything but.

What is less efficient than the story of mankind? If it were about efficiency, God would have wiped the plate clean and commenced with more promising subjects. The Bible in entirety is a love story, a tale of unquenchable delight—His for us, finally ours for Him. No sound rule of parenting is modeled in the sprint of an old man down the road to meet his prodigal. Only delight. No royal protocol is modeled in the dance of a half-naked king before his subjects and the Lord with all his might. Only delight. What is more useless than hymns?

"Let the mind for an instant consider the history of the Redeemer's love, and a thousand enchanting acts of affection will suggest themselves. . . . Our souls may well faint for joy . . . for our loving benefactor Jesus Christ our Lord, whose love is wonderful, passing the love of women" (C.H. Spurgeon).

OH, FOR A THOUSAND TONGUES

If you wish to abide in Jesus, it is important to pray constantly and to be in His word. When the flesh makes it hard to pray and read, I find that it is never hard to sing a hymn. Walking the dog and weary of my prayer list, I suddenly remember a melody and climb up on my Father's lap, as it were, and serenade Him. Where is the man so brutish that he does not like to sing?

And this is not cheating; it is the gift of God to the prayer challenged ("addressing one another with psalms and hymns and spiritual songs," Ephesians 5:19). And so is Charles Wesley a gift, whose songs in the night (and sometimes his spiritual night) have bequeathed to us the best of both prayer and the meat of His word.

December 18th is the 300th anniversary of that "other" Wesley, John's younger brother, 18th born child of Samuel and Susanna—and as good a pro-life argument as you will adduce. In North Lincolnshire, England, this year a gala flower festival held "Wesley Day" on May 24, to their credit, finding the "born again" date of the brothers a marker more important than the "born of woman" statistic interesting to bibliographers.

Though known as the co-founder with John of Methodism, it is from "methods" that Charles was delivered that spring of 1738, from a spiritual halfway house of sincere but legalistic religion without much heart. The Moravians provided the heart. Peter Bohler, of that German pietistic sect, like a Priscilla and Aquilla to Apollos's inchoate faith, introduced Charles to the grace note of joy and true evangelicalism. And oh how those Moravians could sing!

An entry in Charles's diary penned at the home of a Moravian brother: "I now found myself at peace with God and rejoiced in hope of loving Christ. . . . I saw that by faith I stood, by the continual support of faith. . . . I went to bed still sensible of my own weakness . . . yet confident of Christ's protection."

It was the next day that Charles began to write the first of a torrent of hymns, his occluded heart at long last unblocked by gospel grace, releasing rivers of the Holy Spirit. It was three days later that brother John was enraptured through the selfsame salvation door at a meeting of Moravians where Martin Luther's Epistle to the Romans was read. He reported feeling "strangely warmed."

The circuit rider (John) and the hymn writer (Charles), thus anointed, and joined in the joyful obsession by George Whitefield (whose own quickening came in 1735), proceeded to preach wherever they could find an ear to hear—in open fields and prisons and to the soot-streaked faces of coal miners moved to tears. Under the expanse of sky they would meet their throngs when Anglican church doors were slammed on them. "Therefore let us go to Him outside the camp and bear the reproach He endured" (Hebrews 13:13).

We are wont to erect monuments to the great faith heroes of old, each claiming them for our own, now that they are dead and nonthreatening—though I wonder if I, back in the 18th century, would have been willing to "bear the reproach" of a madman for Christ, wet with the dew of outdoor preaching. ("Ashamed. I hear my mocking voice call out among the scoffers"—to quote a hymn not written by Charles Wesley.)

As my own personal acknowledgment of the tercentennial, I decided to read through Wesley's hymns. Not all 6,500 of them but the ones that have risen to the top like farm cream. I was looking for the soul of the man, a more direct pipeline than biographers could give. I discerned that a Christian three centuries and an ocean apart was just like me and sang to Jesus because he needed to:

"Jesus! The name that charms our fears.
That bids our sorrows cease;
'Tis music in the sinner's ears,
'Tis life, and health, and peace.

"He breaks the power of canceled sin,
He sets the prisoner free;
His blood can make the foulest clean;
His blood availed for me."

Hymns are good because when I'm singing, I'm not sinning. The fact is that without them, even walking the dog in the morning can be a hazardous occupation.

AMEN! PREACH IT!

When I was in seminary in the late '70s, there was precisely one black student, named Carl Ellis, and he pretty much saved my seminary experience. Here we were folded into rows in the auditorium, a sea of unrelieved whiteness and looking for all the world like Pop minus the pitchfork in *American Gothic*. There was the professor at the front, telling us interesting things about Parmenides and God. Then from the dimly lit bleachers came the husky African-American voice—unabashed, uncorkable: "Amen!" "Uh-huh!" "Preach it!"

Brothers, in those spontaneous emissions was redemption. Remove them and you had . . . a lecture. Retain them and you had connectivity, relevance—worship. The Godward praises of my neighbor are contagious.

Another professor punctuated erudite exposition

on Revelation with a cappella eruptions of "Worthy is the Lamb." There was a twinge of awkwardness in the student body (mine) that was not accustomed to mixing academics with praise songs. Sisters, why would a person be embarrassed to mix academics with praise songs?

This is a paean to all the folks who praise at inappropriate times. They know no compartments between praise and lectures, between praise and chatting afterwards at the café. They waste scads of time at their carrels in the library stopping over every other sentence of Van Til to praise their glorious God.

And when it comes to that, I have noticed that nothing I ever do non-interactively ever sticks. At any given moment that my religious activities become mere doctrine and not communion with Jesus, I have, for that moment at least, stepped out of truly biblical Christian living into some other mode of being—judge, spectator, player at religion. Francis Schaeffer said true spirituality "is a moment-by-moment, increasing, experiential relationship to Christ" (*True Spirituality*). Where have you gone, brother?

I'm not a Skinnerian, but I'll share a new habit that has changed my life. No more do I listen to the Sunday sermon in passive entertainment mode, one cylinder firing. I have taken to muttering through the sermon. When the preacher says Jesus died for my sins, I find myself whispering, "Praise you, Jesus!"—and it's OK if someone overhears me. When he says Jesus has been exalted to the Father's side and handed authority for the church, I may let escape something greedy like, "Lord, open the floodgates!" Interactive listening just feels right, completing the circle from God's mouth to my heart and back to God's ears.

The hymns are no longer a warm-up act for the sermon. Nor time for taking mental inventory of what's in the freezer. It was when I finally set my mind to focus on every word of the worship songs that I realized how much I wasn't doing it before. I am learning to sing like my Lover is near. I send up thank-yous in the half-note rests to make the words my own. Today I caught myself raising my hands at a lyric that said, "I lift up my hands to you." Pardon my moment of rapturous abandon.

When the benediction is pronounced, it doesn't sound like the closing protocol of Robert's Rules of Order anymore. I claim it and am still thinking about the words hours later. They were prayed over me by an ordained man, so I expect them to have gone out with power. The parson says, "Now to Him who is able to keep you from falling," and I echo in my spirit, "Lord, You will keep me from falling." The parson says, "to present you before His glorious presence without fault and with great joy," and I take it to the bank. I insist on what's mine. Christ won it; I want it.

It's bad enough our psyches have those rigid rows of pews to contend with, a long way from the Corinthian house church where young Eutychus slouched on the window sill, and I'll bet there was a fair amount of Carl Ellis holy rambunctiousness. I don't know what Frank Lloyd Wright says about the interplay of architecture and the soul, but I worry. And I find myself leaning hard against losing Christ in Christian traditions, which C.S. Lewis called "the subtlest of all the snares." I have no solutions but to pull like mad in the opposite direction, for a moment-by-moment faith, worship, and love.

Maybe one of you could shout "Amen!"

HOLIDAY AND HEAVEN

Once you cross from north to south of Cheltenham Avenue into Philadelphia proper, the names of the churches go from the sedate to the sleeved up: Better Way Bible Church, Bible Deliverance Holiness Church, Abundant Life Healing Fellowship Church, Turning Point Worship Center, Solid Rock Fellowship. I've been wanting to go there.

Today after the first service at sedate I slipped out the side door with MapQuest directions and crossed the line. I had phoned Vision of Missions on North 11th Street and inquired as to worship times. The receptionist chuckled and said, "We start at 11, but I can't tell you when we finish." I was sold.

Churches south of the border don't look like churches, which is all to the good—once you can find them. You slow your car to a crawl in the mainly deserted streets where Sunday morning shakes her skirts of all hangover-nursers and leaves the salt of the earth and the children of light. You look for storefronts, not steeples.

> "I shuffle down past the Third Street Gospel Mission;
> Jesus always saves a place there just for me.
> He's got his own band of angels playin' music.
> From a block away you can hear them sing
> To a kick drum and a tambourine.
> Corner of Holiday and Heaven,
> No place on earth I'd rather be."

This is my second time, so I know what to expect. A lady will start chanting "Hallelujah" into one of the five mikes at the front of the room, to no perceptible cue. People will slowly gravitate to seats. In a few minutes the mikes and chairs will fill in, the "Hallelujah!" taking on a life of its own and swelling toward crescendo. It will pick up a single electric guitar along the way, then the bass when it feels like it, and finally keyboard and drum.

The gathering river of "Hallelujah!" now branches into rivulets of simple lyrics dwelling on His awesomeness and majesty and holiness. Like Bolero but with Holy Spirit fire for fuel, it sweeps all in its path into a trance of praise. The whole church sways now, though you don't recall where it began. A half-hour in, there is no sign of the song subsiding.

"Now from the outside looks like
Just another lonely place
On just another hard road downtown,
Where the wind blows the trash around
In circles on dirty streets.
But the joy of the Lord is found
Where the heart of the new believers beat.
Corner of Holiday and Heaven,
No place on earth I'd rather be."

I don't know what the Regulative Principle of Worship is that I was supposed to learn in seminary, but I'm pretty sure by now it's been gagged and hogtied and tossed out the window. Five ladies in floor-length white robes looking like angels come up and dance to the glory of God, waving colorful, sheer kerchiefs in pantomime to a song about finding a secret place with the Lord. Ulrich Zwingli might faint.

The preacher comes up, almost anticlimactically. He holds no paper or 3-by-5 card, and it is clear he will not be contained by the pulpit area. His text is Hebrews

4 and Psalm 119 but he hardly gets to the Psalm, detoured by the Holy Spirit into words earmarked for me from the foundation of the world, though everyone in the joint is resonating, too, urging him loquaciously with "Come ons" and "Hallelujahs" and "Praise Jesus" and "Glory!" as he wipes his brow at intervals and takes no prisoners.

I wish it would never end. Hey Lord, let's build three booths and stay—one for you and one for Moses and one for Elijah. There's quarreling and kids with epilepsy down there. Couldn't we linger a while in your house? One more round of "Hallelujah"?

> "Goin' down to let my light shine through a
> lonely window.
> A chance a lost soul will face up to the pain.
> I like the preachin' . . . that little dance he does
> so entertainin'.
> He seems to know just how to save my soul,
> Take my burdens, make me whole.
> Corner of Holiday and Heaven,
> No place on earth I'd rather be.
> Right there on Holiday and Heaven,
> No place on earth I'd rather be"
> (Bryan Duncan, "Joyride").

UNQUENCHABLE OPTIMISM

I recall my first experience with the Korean shoe custom. It was 1979, for I was not yet married to my Asian husband. About to enter the apartment of a couple he knew, I stood at the door sizing up the situation: Everyone inside was shoeless; neatly paired footwear sat at the threshold; I was a first-time visitor. As a friendly voice within beckoned me enter, I made a split-second calculation—and guessed wrong. I plowed into the house with shod feet, thus desecrating the showroom-pristine carpeting.

In ignorance of Korean culture from the inside, I had erroneously ascribed to the shoe rule a significance of which I was quickly disabused. I had made the assumption that the removal of foot apparel was: (1) a mystical practice rising from the mists of Oriental history; (2) an honor reserved for family and close friends. Come to find out the purpose is to keep the rugs clean.

Things always look different from the inside than the outside. Everyone remembers being a high-school freshman and gazing up through cirrus clouds to senior nirvana, only to discover three years later that it wasn't what you thought. Fifty-five years old looks nothing like it did when I was 20, now that I inhabit it.

C.S. Lewis, a self-described "middle-aged moralist" addressing an assembly of graduates, warned of the dangers of wanting too badly to be "insiders" of a certain kind: "Your pleasure will be short-lived. The circle cannot have from within the charm it had from outside. By the very act of admitting you it has lost its magic." (Groucho Marx: "I don't want to be in a club that would have me as a member.")

Mexico or Mauritania are just useless coordinates on a world map until you meet a Mexican or Mauritanian and are fond of him. All at once the whole country is beautiful.

A perennial question I have is whether I see a matter more clearly when I just know "the facts" or when I know the person to whom the facts pertain. Is relationship an inhibitor or enhancer of good judgment? Does being "in love" distort vision? Lady

Justice dons a blindfold and scales, signifying that justice is no respecter of persons (Leviticus 19:15; Exodus 23:8). I have a friend who wants a divorce, and I have more sympathy than if she were a "case study" on paper. Am I too sympathetic? Has friendship blinded me?

Eve wanted to be an insider to the most prestigious Inside in the universe—the Trinity. The Serpent promised an insider's perspective on "good and evil." She got it, but it didn't look the same from the inside as she'd hoped while on the outside. Adultery sometimes looks appealing from the outside, but the view from the inside is of a hotel for the dead (Proverbs 9:18). Sin looks like freedom (Jeremiah 2:31) till you find yourself its slave (John 8:34).

In *The Voyage of the Dawn Treader,* Lucy came upon a Magic Book and tried a spell "which would let you know what your friends thought about you." Some inside knowledge is better not had (Ecclesiastes 7:21-22).

On the other hand, a man cannot be a good husband unless he has tried to get inside his wife's head. This will be culture shock as severe as any trip to Mexico or Mauritania, but worth the journey (1 Peter 3:7).

A Popeye cartoon that captivated me in the early '60s was of our unlikely hero dashing for cover into a small tent in the desert, only to discover, once inside, an impossibly palatial celestry dripping with jewels and treasure. The delightful dissonance of small outsides and large insides prepared me for a lifetime of similar surprises.

The Christian life looks boring and constricted to outsiders. But open the door and it ushers into room after room of delights.

One of the best things that's happened to me in the last three years is finding Christians from Christ's other "fold" (John 10:16). They talk differently, they notice Scriptures that slipped my net, they sing different songs in a different tempo on different instruments. They have unquenchable optimism. Praising the Lord with a heart enthralled with Him once looked, from the outside, like fanaticism (ask David the King). But it sure does look different from the inside.

ABOUT THE AUTHOR

Andrée Seu began writing almost 20 years ago after an aspiring writer moved in next door. On the occasion of her daughter's shedding a baby tooth, her neighbor dropped a poem in her mailbox. Andrée cried on the spot at the sheer beauty of it. Encouraged, her young neighbor started writing more and depositing poems, then essays, then short stories on the porch after dark. This "box" tradition continued for a few years and became Andrée's personal school of writing. Beth Kephart went on to be a semi-finalist for the National Book Award for her book *A Slant of Sun*.

Andrée Seu is a senior writer for *WORLD Magazine*, the author of *Won't Let You Go Unless You Bless Me* and *Normal Kingdom Business*. She lives and writes from Philadelphia.